To Issy,
HAPPY 21st BIRTHDAY!!
Hope this gives you
some inspo for isaHells
kitchen!!
Lots of Love
Annabel xxx

GW00656484

Vegan
BUDDHA BOWLS

MORE THAN
50
HEALTHY AND
SUSTAINABLE
RECIPES

JESSICA LERCHENMÜLLER

Vegan
BUDDHA BOWLS

MORE THAN 50 HEALTHY AND
SUSTAINABLE RECIPES

GRUB STREET | LONDON

CONTENTS

ALL IN THE ONE BOWL

Mealtimes are a wonderful opportunity to sit down together at the table and enjoy good food made using fresh ingredients. They don't always have to feature intricate dishes and exotic products. Here, we offer simple and colourful, everyday dishes made from a combination of plant-based ingredients chosen according to preference to make a hearty meal in a bowl.

When it comes to finding the ingredients, you have the whole world to choose from. They can include rice, bananas and pak choi from far away, and potatoes, apples or beetroot from local farms. Attitudes towards nutrition and the importance of where food is sourced have essentially changed in recent years. Many people have discovered an enthusiasm for cooking their own meals and attach greater importance to a balanced diet. In the process, some have come to acknowledge the diversity of plant-based diets and embarked on a culinary journey through the incredible variety of vegan flavours. This has inevitably led them to discover the one-bowl vegan meal.

Buddha bowls are more than just a trend; they are arguably the most creative way to combine indulgence and wellness in a single meal. The different ingredients can be combined with each other depending on your mood and individually chosen to meet your nutritional requirements. Grains, crunchy vegetables, long-forgotten varieties of pulses and crunchy toppings can go together to create lots of healthy, everyday dishes. From breakfast to dinner, from quick and easy individual bowls to intimate sharing bowls for casual cooking nights with friends, this book of vegan Buddha bowl recipes will excite anybody who craves healthy comfort food featuring spices and flavours from around the world.

All recipes serve two people.

ICONS

 THE TIME IT TAKES UNTIL THE BOWL IS READY TO SERVE

 TIMING WHERE MOST OF THE COOKING IS DONE IN THE OVEN

VEGAN IS ANYTHING BUT BORING

Never before have we had access to such a wide variety of foods sourced locally and from around the globe as we do today. However, just by sticking to five food groups – fruits, vegetables, whole grains, pulses, seeds and nuts – you can take full advantage of them. A vegan diet is anything but boring. It's actually a culinary experience filled with nutrients, surprises and taste sensations.

WHY IS IT CALLED A **BUDDHA BOWL?**

Buddha bowls have been providing us with extraordinary flavour experiences for a number of years now. Whether it's breakfast, lunch or dinner, these hearty bowls are the perfect way to try new and healthy pleasures.

But how did the Buddha bowl get its name? While the bowl part is easy enough, the word 'Buddha' is a Sanskrit word meaning 'the awakened one'. However, this literal translation has little to do with the colourful trend that started in the United States and how it got its name. Instead, the term is believed to have come from the likeness of the bowl to a Buddha belly – when viewed from the front with its brimming contents, the bowl appears to bulge like a Buddha belly.

However, the explanation offered by ōryōki, the food ritual of the Zen Buddhist tradition, is perhaps less far-fetched. This ritual involves eating from bowls of different sizes. The largest bowls are also referred to Buddha bowls by the Zen monks.

GOOD REASONS TO LOVE VEGAN BUDDHA BOWLS

Creativity knows no limits when you prepare vegan Buddha bowls. The combinations of different ingredients can depend on your mood. The choice of different fruits and vegetables can vary with the changing seasons, while the grains, nuts and seeds can also be replaced according to personal taste. Suddenly, you'll find you have a new and nutritious taste sensation in the bowl.

MACRONUTRIENTS

The three macronutrients are carbohydrates, proteins and fats. They are the main source of nutrients in our food and provide our bodies with the energy it needs to function.

Carbohydrates

Carbohydrates usually make up the largest part of our diet – about a half to one-third. They contain complex sugar molecules, which is the fuel our body requires to supply energy to our cells. A distinction can be made between short-chain and long-chain carbohydrates. The longer the carbohydrate chain, the longer it takes to break down its component molecules and absorb them into the bloodstream. While short-chain carbohydrates cause blood sugar levels to rise quickly, long-chain carbohydrates provide our body with a sustained energy supply. These include:

- Pulses (lentils, chickpeas, etc.)
- Potatoes
- Fruits
- Quinoa
- Rice
- Dried fruits
- Granary bread

Proteins

Proteins consist of different building blocks called amino acids. These are involved in a range of important bodily processes, such as cell growth. Of the twenty essential amino acids that exist, more than half are produced by the body itself. The remaining eight are absorbed from food. Not only do they come from meat and fish, which are high in protein, but also from a large number of plant-based foods, which our body processes in the same way as it does animal products. These include:

- Beans, chickpeas, lentils
- Pumpkin seeds, hemp seeds, chia seeds, almonds, cashew nuts, hazelnuts
- Quinoa, oats, millet, lupin beans
- Soya beans, tofu, tempeh, seitan

Fats

Fats are energy stores and supply building materials for various areas of the body. Excess energy is stored by the body in the form of fat. Fats play an important role in supplying material for the process of cell formation. The actual cell membrane consists of fat. In addition, some vitamins are exclusively fat-soluble, which means that they can only be absorbed and processed by the body in combination with fats. While healthy fats have a major role in certain important processes in the body, processed and hydrogenated fats can cause long-term harm. Many different plant-based foods contain healthy fats, including omega-6 fatty acids. These are typically present in animal fats, but our requirements can be easily met with a plant-based diet. For instance, they are present in many oils, such as sesame oil, soya oil and sunflower oil. Omega-3 fatty acids, on the other hand, are often lacking in a vegan diet. However, this requirement can still be met quite easily by taking one teaspoon of linseed oil or hemp oil. These include:

- Avocado
- Olives
- Nuts and seeds

MICRONUTRIENTS

Micronutrients are also known as trace elements. These include both vitamins and minerals. Unlike macronutrients, micronutrients are only needed in small amounts, but they are just as essential for healthy bodily function, for example, to protect our cells and for healthy skin, hair and nail growth. Micronutrients cannot be produced by the body itself and must be taken in through food. Our daily intake of micronutrients depends on our age, gender and lifestyle.

Calcium

Calcium is an important nutrient for bones and teeth. It also plays an important role in the functioning of muscles, nerves, blood clotting and hormone secretion.

- Sources include kale, spinach, Swiss chard, haricot beans, almonds, sesame seeds and tofu

Zinc

Zinc is required by the body to metabolise proteins and for a healthy immune system and good eyesight.

- Sources include whole grains, pulses, oats, pumpkin seeds, peanuts and Brazil nuts

Iodine

Iodine is essential for the thyroid hormone. This hormone is needed by our body for bone development and to metabolise macronutrients.

- Sources include seaweed, table salt, mushrooms, broccoli and peanuts

Iron

Iron is responsible for the transport of oxygen in the body as well as for the process by which energy is supplied to our cells.

- Sources include amaranth, quinoa, lentils, kidney beans, sesame seeds, sunflower seeds, cardamom and cinnamon

Selenium

Selenium maintains a healthy immune system and is important for detoxification processes in the body. It also has an antioxidant effect and supports the production of thyroid hormones.

- Sources include Brazil nuts, cashew nuts, sunflower seeds, coconut, oats, rice, mushrooms, lentils, broccoli and haricot beans

Vitamin B

Vitamin B is the name of a group comprising eight vitamins. Our requirements for most of these can be met by a plant-based diet. However, there are no reliable plant sources for vitamin B_{12} and it is typically supplied as a food supplement. Vitamin B_{12} is needed for the DNA synthesis as well as for the formation of new proteins.

- Sources include pulses, bananas, spinach, peas, lentils, kale, broccoli, sesame seeds and sunflower seeds

THE HIGHLIGHT OF A BOWL: THE TOPPING

SWEET TOPPINGS

Nuts (roasted, chopped or ground)

- Including cashew nuts, hazelnuts, almonds, macadamia nuts, Brazil nuts and pecan nuts enhanced with maple syrup, cinnamon, or vanilla

Seeds (roasted or ground)

- Including buckwheat, hemp seeds, pumpkin seeds, linseed, sesame seeds, sunflower seeds enhanced with maple syrup, cinnamon or vanilla

Dried fruits

- Includes apricots, dates, figs, goji berries, raspberries and mangoes

Seasonal fruits

- Including apple and pear wedges, banana slices, berries

Granola (e.g. see page 14)

Stewed fruits, jam, nut and seed butters

Spices

- Including baking cocoa, gingerbread spice mix, cinnamon

SPICY TOPPINGS

Nuts (roasted, chopped or ground)

- Including cashew nuts, hazelnuts, almonds, macadamia nuts, Brazil nuts and pecan nuts enhanced with salt, pepper and spices

Seeds (roasted or ground)

- Including buckwheat, hemp seeds, pumpkin seeds, linseed, sesame seeds and sunflower seeds enhanced with salt, pepper and dried herbs

Sprouts

- Including bean sprouts, garden cress

Spicy Granola (e.g. see page 14)

Dips (e.g. see pages 20–23)

Spices

- Including chilli flakes, garlic powder and herb salt

TOPPING RECIPES

ALMOND AND CINNAMON GRANOLA

INGREDIENTS

3 tbsp coconut oil

3 tbsp maple syrup

2 tbsp almond butter

3 tbsp hulled hemp seeds

200 g jumbo rolled oats

50 g spelt flakes

100 g blanched almonds

1 tbsp ground cinnamon

METHOD

1 Preheat the oven to 180°C and line a baking tray with baking parchment. Mix together the coconut oil, maple syrup and almond paste in a small bowl. Combine the hemp seeds, rolled oats, spelt flakes, almonds and cinnamon in a large bowl, add the wet ingredients and mix thoroughly.

2 Transfer the mixture to the baking tray and lightly press together with your hands, which will later leave small and crispy clusters. Spread the mixture evenly in the tray and bake for about 25 minutes, until golden brown. Stir with a wooden spoon after about 10 minutes. Then remove from oven, leave to cool and store in a large, airtight jar.

 TIP

For a savoury alternative, replace the cinnamon and maple syrup with half a teaspoon of salt and half a teaspoon of the herbs of your choice.

ROASTED NUTS

MAPLE AND CINNAMON CANDIED NUTS

INGREDIENTS

200 g mixed nuts and seeds
   of choice

1 tbsp ground cinnamon

3 tbsp maple syrup

Salt

METHOD

1   Roast the nuts and seeds in a dry frying pan over a
    medium heat for about 7 minutes, stirring constantly.
    Lower the heat after 5 minutes. Then stir in the
    cinnamon, maple syrup and a pinch of salt and
    continue to roast for 2 more minutes. Leave the
    mixture to cool and then store in an airtight jar.

SALTED AND SPICED NUTS

INGREDIENTS

200 g mixed nuts and seeds
   of choice

½ tsp salt

1 tsp spices (e.g. curry, garlic
   powder)

METHOD

2   Roast the nuts and seeds in a dry frying pan over a
    medium heat for about 7 minutes, stirring constantly.
    Lower the heat after 5 minutes. Then stir in the salt and
    spices and continue to roast for 2 more minutes. Leave
    the mixture to cool and then store in an airtight jar.

BUDDHA BOWL BASICS

No matter whether their contents are beautifully arranged or simply thrown together, sweet or savoury, Buddha bowls have one thing in common: they're colourful, flavourful, satisfying and healthy. Grains and pulses are the basic ingredients of vegan Buddha bowls. These are complemented by a wide variety of fruits and vegetables. Nuts, seeds and sprouts are popular toppings and provide nutrients in addition to flavour and texture.

CEREALS AND PSEUDOCEREALS

Simply referred to as grains, cereals and pseudocereals are among the most important staple foods and supply the energy we need with every meal. They are high in essential nutrients, including dietary fibre, proteins, vitamins and minerals. Grains can be combined in many ways, which in the case of vegan Buddha bowls, can provide a welcome change. So instead of rice, you can just as easily use quinoa or couscous.

BASIC METHOD: PREPARE CEREALS AND PSEUDOCEREALS PROPERLY

Preparation

1. Put the grains into a fine-mesh sieve and rinse them under the tap until the water runs clear. As you rinse, rub the grains together with your hand in a clockwise direction. This removes any impurities and excess starch. Then drain well.

2. Put the washed grains into a sealable jar and cover with the same amount of warm water as required for cooking. Add a tablespoon of apple cider vinegar and soak for 8–24 hours, ideally overnight. Then drain and rinse the grain again in a fine-mesh sieve.

3. Now add plenty of water with a pinch of salt to a suitably sized pan and bring to the boil. The recommended ratio is a quarter of a teaspoon of salt to 100 ml of water.

Bring the salted water to the boil, lower the heat and stir in the grain. Cover the pan with a lid and cook according to instructions on the package. Just before the end of the cooking time, remove the pan from the heat and leave to stand for 4–5 more minutes before serving.

 TIP:

Unlike pulses, grains don't necessarily need to be soaked before cooking. However, soaking is recommended because it breaks down proteins that are difficult to digest, removes phytic acid and significantly reduces cooking time. Phytic acid actually prevents certain minerals contained in cereals from being absorbed by the body.

This is an easy and optimum way to prepare the following grains:

- Amaranth
- Buckwheat
- Couscous
- Spelt
- Barley
- Oats
- Millet
- Polenta and cornmeal
- Quinoa
- Rice

PULSES

Pulses are rich in high-quality proteins, satiating dietary fibre, minerals and complex carbohydrates. They are good for intestinal health as well as lowering cholesterol and preventing cardiovascular problems. Pulses provide a plentiful supply of vitamins C, B_1 and B_6, iron, copper, magnesium, manganese, zinc and phosphorus. Daily protein requirements can also be met by incorporating enough pulses into your everyday diet, making them particularly appropriate for plant-based diets. However, certain things should be taken into consideration when using dried beans, chickpeas or lentils.

BASIC METHOD: PREPARE PULSES PROPERLY

Buying pulses

Preference should be given to pulses with organic certification because their shape and colour are indicators of quality. They should always be evenly sized, clean and undamaged. Even small stones in the package can be a sign of poor quality.

Preparation

1. Put the desired amount of pulses into a sieve or colander and rinse them under the tap until the water runs clear.

2. Then transfer them to a pan together with plenty of warm water. The heat dissolves the largely indigestible starch in the pulses. General rule: Add a tablespoon of apple cider vinegar for every 100 g of pulses and soak for 8–12 hours, ideally overnight.

3. Drain. Combine the pulses in a pan together with enough cold water, bring to the boil and skim off the froth. Then lower the heat and simmer until the pulses are soft. As salt can slow the cooking process, wait until about 10 minutes before the end of the cooking time to stir in a tablespoon of salt for every 100 g of pulses.

4. Then drain and rinse the pulses with clean water before continuing with the recipe.

Soaking time

Broad beans	overnight (8–12 hours)
Brown lentils	1 hour (not strictly necessary)
Peas	overnight (8–12 hours)
Beans (general)	overnight (8–12 hours)
Yellow lentils	No soaking required
Green lentils	1 hour (not strictly necessary)
Chickpeas	overnight (8–12 hours)
Kidney beans	overnight (8–12 hours)
Mung beans	overnight (8–12 hours)
Red lentils	No soaking required
Black (beluga) lentils	No soaking required
Soya beans	overnight (8–12 hours)
Haricot beans	overnight (8–12 hours)

NUTS AND SEEDS

Nuts and seeds are small nutrient factories filled with healthy unsaturated fatty acids that protect against cardiovascular disease. They also contain large amounts of zinc, selenium and other important trace elements that strengthen our immune system. And if that weren't enough, they provide plenty of protein, minerals and dietary fibre, which are good for muscle development, strong bones and good digestion. These little powerhouses not only enrich simple dishes but also add heavenly flavour. What's more, nuts and seeds can be used to make fantastic dairy alternatives and spreads.

- Cashew nuts
- Chia seeds
- Hulled hemp seeds
- Hazelnuts
- Pumpkin seeds
- Linseed
- Almonds
- Poppy seeds
- Brazil nuts
- Sesame seeds
- Sunflower seeds
- Walnuts

BREAKFAST:
Dairy alternatives from nuts, seeds and grains

Because you choose a vegan diet doesn't mean doing without; rather, it's a matter of healthy choice and variety. Supermarket dairy alternative aisles showcase a wide range of products made from a wide variety of ingredients, such as soya, almonds and even buckwheat. While the possibilities seem endless, making them in your own kitchen is a breeze.

Note: When making nut milks (e.g. almond or hazelnut), always use blanched nuts.

Preparation

- The recommended ratio is one litre of water for every 100 g of nuts, seeds or grains (e.g. buckwheat).

- Combine the desired amount of nuts, seeds or grains with a pinch of salt in a sealable jar and soak overnight (if using oats, only soak for 20–30 minutes). Soaking breaks down phytic acid and neutralizes enzyme inhibitors for better absorption of vitamins, minerals and proteins.

- Then drain, rinse well and transfer the nuts, seeds or grains to a powerful blender together with a quarter of a teaspoon of salt. Add cinnamon, dates or honey to taste and add about a litre of water. Blend on the highest speed for 1–2 minutes.

- Strain the liquid by squeezing through a nut milk bag or muslin. If your blender is powerful enough, you can skip this step and pour the milk directly through a funnel into a glass bottle. The plant-based milk will keep in the refrigerator for 2–3 days.

BREAKFAST, LUNCH & DINNER:
Nut and seed butters at every meal

Home-made nut and seed butters taste simply fabulous! Soups, salads, stews and breakfast bowls can become taste sensations when enhanced with almond or sesame butter. All you need is a good food processor or a powerful blender (a hand-held blender isn't suitable because it does not have the necessary power).

BASIC RECIPE: NUT OR SEED BUTTER

INGREDIENTS

200 g nuts (e.g. almonds, cashews or hazelnuts) or seeds (e.g. sesame) of your choice

METHOD

1 Roast the nuts or seeds in the oven at 160°C or in a dry frying pan over a medium heat for 10–12 minutes. Leave to cool completely.

2 Transfer the nuts or seeds to a food processor or powerful blender and grind for several minutes. Stop every so often to allow the appliance to cool down a little, and scrape down the sides with a spoon. Repeat the process until you obtain a runny paste with a creamy consistency.

 TIP

Combine different nuts and seeds for a special experience. You can also season your nut to enhance the flavour (e.g. by adding a pinch of sea salt, 1–2 teaspoons of ground cinnamon, a little vanilla or 2 tablespoons of maple syrup). Add the seasoning at the end and mix well.

SPREADS & DIPS

GUACAMOLE

INGREDIENTS

1 avocado

1 lemon

1 tsp maple syrup

Salt

1 pinch garlic powder
(optional)

1 pinch chilli flakes (optional)

METHOD

1 Halve the avocado and remove the stone. Use a spoon to scoop out the flesh and put it into a small bowl. Mash the avocado with a fork. Squeeze the lemon. Add the lemon juice and maple syrup to the avocado and mix to a creamy consistency. Season with the salt. Add garlic powder and/or a few chilli flakes if desired.

PLAIN HUMMUS

INGREDIENTS

1 tin chickpeas (about 240 g
drained weight)

1 lemon

2 tbsp olive oil

1 tsp maple syrup

1 tbsp sesame butter (tahini)

¼ tsp ground coriander

¼ tsp garlic powder

1 pinch chilli flakes

Salt

METHOD

1 To make the hummus, drain the chickpeas from the tin. Rinse, drain and put them into a bowl. Squeeze the lemon and add the juice to the chickpeas together with the remaining ingredients and 2 tablespoons of water. Blend to a creamy consistency in a blender or with a hand-held blender. Season with salt.

2 Transfer the hummus to an airtight jar and seal tightly. It will keep in the refrigerator for 1 week.

BEETROOT HUMMUS

INGREDIENTS

150 g beetroot

1 batch plain hummus
(see page 20)

METHOD

1 Peel the beetroot, combine with the hummus and blend to a creamy consistency in a blender, or in a bowl with a hand-held blender.

CURRIED SWEET POTATO HUMMUS

INGREDIENTS

150 g sweet potatoes

1 tbsp olive oil

½ tsp curry powder

1 batch plain hummus
(see page 20)

METHOD

1 Preheat the oven to 180°C and line an ovenproof dish with baking parchment. Peel and cut the sweet potato into small cubes, then put into the dish and drizzle with the olive oil. Bake for 20–25 minutes, take out and then leave to cool down a little.

2 Combine the baked sweet potato cubes with the curry powder and hummus, and blend to a creamy consistency in a blender, or in a bowl with a hand-held blender.

MORE DIP IDEAS

YOGHURT DIP

INGREDIENTS

½ lemon

150 g vegan yoghurt alternative (e.g. coconut, almond, soya)

1 tsp maple syrup

Salt and pepper

1 pinch chilli flakes (optional)

METHOD

1   Squeeze the lemon. Combine half the juice in a bowl with the remaining ingredients and mix thoroughly. Season with a pinch each of salt and pepper, and add a few chilli flakes if desired.

 TIP

Stir in a tablespoon of medium-strength mustard to give the dip a little kick.

ORIENTAL DIP

INGREDIENTS

¼ ripe banana

1 tbsp sesame butter (tahini)

½ tsp curry powder

1 batch yoghurt dip (see above)

METHOD

1   Peel and mash the banana with a fork. Then mix with the yoghurt dip, sesame butter and curry powder.

CASHEW AND CHOCOLATE SPREAD

INGREDIENTS

500 g cashew nuts

35 g dried and pitted
  dates (preferably Medjool)

2 tbsp baking cocoa

2 tbsp coconut oil

Salt

METHOD

1 Roast cashews in a dry frying over a medium heat for about 7 minutes, stirring constantly. After about 5 minutes, lower the heat and continue to roast for 2 more minutes. Remove from the heat and leave to cool a little.

2 Combine the cashews, dates, cocoa, coconut oil and a pinch of salt in a powerful blender and blend until thick and smooth. Stop every so often to allow the appliance to cool down a little, and scrape down the sides with a spoon. It takes a little patience until the spread is at the proper consistency, but the result is definitely worth the effort.

 TIP

Instead of cashews, you can easily use other nuts such as almonds, hazelnuts or macadamia nuts.

VEGAN SALAD DRESSINGS

ASIAN DRESSING

INGREDIENTS

1 clove garlic

1 small piece (about 1 cm) ginger

3 tsp sesame oil

4 tbsp rice vinegar

1 tsp rice syrup

Salt and pepper

METHOD

1 Peel and finely chop the garlic and ginger. Heat 1 tablespoon of oil in a frying pan and fry the garlic and ginger until golden brown. Then combine in a bowl with the remaining ingredients and whisk until fully incorporated.

BALSAMIC VINEGAR DRESSING

INGREDIENTS

3 tbsp balsamic vinegar

2 tbsp olive oil

½ tsp salt

Pepper

METHOD

1 In a bowl, combine the balsamic vinegar, olive oil, salt, and a pinch of pepper with 2 tablespoons of water and whisk until fully incorporated.

APPLE AND MUSTARD DRESSING

INGREDIENTS

2 tbsp apple cider vinegar

2 tbsp olive oil

1 tsp medium-strength
   mustard

1 tsp maple syrup

1 pinch garlic powder
   (optional)

Salt and pepper

METHOD

1 In a bowl, combine the vinegar, olive oil, mustard, maple
   syrup and a pinch each of salt and pepper with 2
   tablespoons of water and a little garlic powder, if desired,
   and whisk until fully incorporated.

LEMON AND MINT DRESSING

INGREDIENTS

¼ bunch fresh mint

1 lemon

4 tbsp olive oil

1 tsp maple syrup

Salt and pepper

METHOD

1 Wash the mint, shake dry, pluck the leaves from the
   stems and finely chop. Squeeze the lemon. In a bowl,
   combine the mint, lemon juice, olive oil, maple syrup and
   a pinch each of salt and pepper with 2 tablespoons of
   water and whisk until fully incorporated.

CREAMY NUT DRESSING

INGREDIENTS

2 limes (or 2 tbsp apple cider
   vinegar)

1 tbsp olive oil

1 tsp cashew butter

1 tsp maple syrup

Salt and pepper

METHOD

1 Squeeze the limes into a bowl and combine with the
   olive oil, cashew butter, maple syrup, a pinch each of salt
   and pepper, and 2 tablespoons of water. Whisk until fully
   incorporated.

BREAKFAST
BOWLS

CREAMY BANANA BOWL
WITH CARAMELISED PEAR WEDGES

INGREDIENTS

FOR THE SMOOTHIE BOWL

2 bananas

90 g millet flakes

4 tbsp almonds (or 2 tbsp almond butter)

8 dried and pitted dates (preferably Medjool)

150 ml almond milk

FOR THE CARAMELISED PEAR

2 tbsp almonds

1 pear

3 tbsp maple syrup

2 tbsp buckwheat

½ tsp ground cinnamon

2 tbsp sesame seeds

EXTRAS

2 tsp maple syrup

METHOD

1 Peel and cut the bananas into large pieces and freeze for at least 2 hours.

2 Use a sharp knife to coarsely chop the almonds. Wash, halve and core the pear. Cut into thin wedges. In a frying pan, combine the chopped almonds, maple syrup, buckwheat, cinnamon and sesame seeds with 2 tablespoons of water, bring to the boil and add the pear slices. Then lower the heat and simmer for 10 minutes, stirring from time to time. Remove from the heat and set aside.

3 To make the smoothie, combine the millet flakes, frozen banana pieces, almonds and dates with the almond milk in a powerful blender and blend to a creamy consistency. Divide the smoothie into two bowls and top with the caramelised pear mixture. Finally, drizzle with a little maple syrup.

 TIP

Add 1 tablespoon of nut butter (see recipe on page 19) for an even more flavourful breakfast bowl.

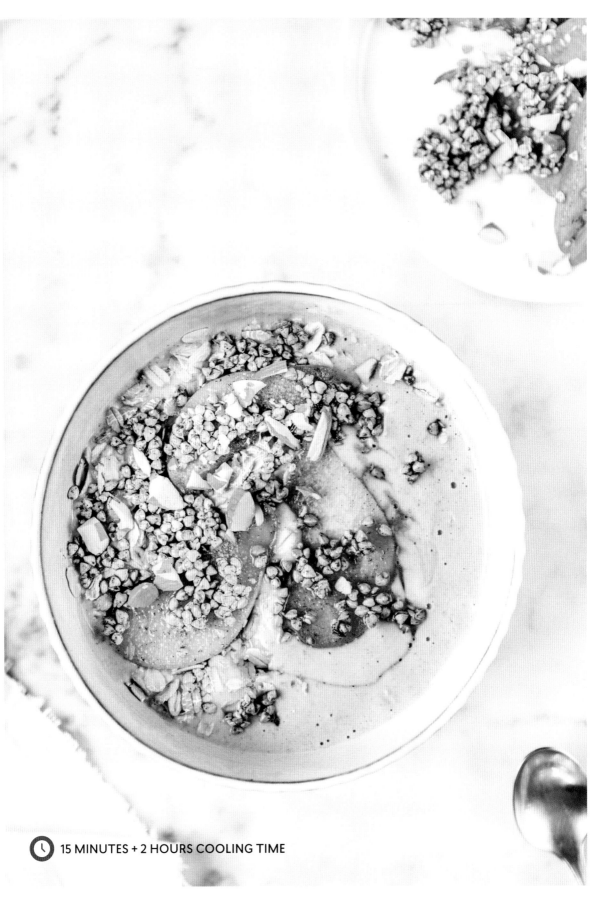

15 MINUTES + 2 HOURS COOLING TIME

OVERNIGHT OATS BOWL
WITH ORANGES AND BLACKBERRIES

INGREDIENTS

FOR THE OVERNIGHT OATS

100 g jumbo rolled oats

2 tbsp ground almonds

1 tbsp cracked linseed

1 tbsp maple syrup

1 pinch Bourbon
    vanilla powder

300 ml almond milk

3 tbsp vegan yoghurt
    alternative (e.g. coconut,
    almond, soya)

EXTRAS

2 small oranges

100 g blackberries

2 tbsp pumpkin seeds

2 tbsp maple syrup

METHOD

1   In a bowl, mix the oats with the ground almonds, linseed, maple syrup, vanilla and almond milk and leave to soak overnight.

2   The next day, peel the oranges, remove the pith and membranes, and thinly slice the flesh. Sort and wash the blackberries and carefully pat them dry. Divide the overnight oats into two bowls and top each with 1 ½ tablespoons yoghurt alternative, orange slices, blackberries, pumpkin seeds and maple syrup.

 TIP

You can replace the fresh fruit with any seasonal varieties. Sunflower seeds also make a great alternative to pumpkin seeds.

15 MINUTES + 12 HOURS SOAKING TIME

PEANUT BUTTER BOWL
WITH SALTED ALMOND BANANA TOPPING

INGREDIENTS

FOR THE SMOOTHIE

2 ripe bananas

7 dried and pitted dates
(preferably Medjool)

2 tbsp coconut flour
(or coconut flakes)

200 ml coconut milk

1 tbsp peanut butter

Sea salt

FOR THE TOPPING

2 dried dates (preferably
Medjool)

2 tbsp almonds

½ banana

EXTRAS

1 tbsp sesame seeds

2 tsp peanut butter

Sea salt

Ground cinnamon

METHOD

1 Peel and cut the bananas into large pieces and freeze for
at least 4 hours.

2 Combine the frozen bananas, dates, coconut flour,
coconut milk, peanut butter and a pinch of sea salt in a
powerful blender and blend to a creamy consistency.
Then divide the smoothie into two bowls.

3 To prepare the topping, slice the dates, coarsely chop
the almonds, and peel and slice the banana lengthways.
Then divide the dates, almonds and banana slices evenly
into the bowls and add half a teaspoon of sesame seeds,
1 teaspoon of peanut butter and a pinch each of sea salt
and cinnamon to each bowl before serving.

 TIP

You can use almond or cashew butter instead of peanut butter.
They are also simple to make yourself (see recipe on page 19).

15 MINUTES + 4 HOURS FREEZING TIME

POPPY SEED PANCAKE BOWL

INGREDIENTS

FOR THE POPPY SEED PANCAKES

2 bananas

200 ml almond milk

4 tbsp maple syrup

2 tbsp coconut oil plus 1 tsp, for cooking

120 g spelt flour

60 g poppy seeds

2 tsp baking powder

Salt

EXTRAS

6 apricots

100 g redcurrants

10 strawberries

4 tbsp vegan yoghurt alternative (e.g. coconut, almond, soya)

2 tbsp apricot jam

2 tbsp maple syrup

2 tsp sesame seeds

METHOD

1 Peel the bananas and mash them in a bowl with a fork. Mix in the almond milk, maple syrup and 2 tablespoons of coconut oil. Then add the flour, poppy seeds, baking powder and a pinch of salt and mix to a smooth batter.

2 Heat the remaining coconut oil in a frying pan. Make a pancake by pouring in 4 tablespoons of batter and cooking on both sides over a medium heat for 2–3 minutes, until golden brown. Repeat the process for the remaining batter.

3 In the meantime, wash, halve and pit the apricots. Then cut the flesh into quarters or wedges. Sort and wash the redcurrant clusters and carefully pat them dry. Then separate the berries. Hull, wash and slice the strawberries lengthways.

4 Stack 4 pancakes in each of two bowls and add half the fresh fruit to each. Garnish each bowl with 2 tablespoons of yoghurt alternative, 1 tablespoon of jam, 1 tablespoon of maple syrup and 1 teaspoon of poppy seeds.

 TIP

For a nuttier version, you can replace the poppy seeds with ground hazelnuts. The fruits can also be replaced with seasonal varieties.

30 MINUTES

BALANCED MORNING BOWL

WITH HEMP SEEDS AND COCONUT YOGHURT

INGREDIENTS

FOR THE MUESLI

3 tbsp chopped almonds

2 tbsp hemp seeds

2 tbsp chia seeds

3 tbsp coconut chips

250 ml almond milk

1 tbsp maple syrup

EXTRAS

200 g coconut yoghurt
    alternative

2 tbsp almonds

50 g blueberries

50 g raspberries

2 tsp strawberry jam

2 tbsp coconut chips

4 mint leaves

2 edible flowers

1 tbsp maple syrup

METHOD

1 To prepare the muesli, mix the dry ingredients in a bowl. Add the almond milk and maple syrup, mix and rest for at least 15 minutes, or preferably cover and rest overnight.

2 Divide the yoghurt alternative and muesli into two bowls. Coarsely chop the almonds. Sort the berries, wash and carefully pat dry. Add the almonds and berries to the bowls together with the jam, coconut chips, washed mint leaves and the flowers. Finally, drizzle with a little maple syrup and serve.

 TIP

You can replace the berries with other seasonal fruits, such as fresh peaches, and you can replace the strawberry jam with apricot jam.

20 MINUTES + 15 MINUTES SOAKING TIME

EASY BREAKFAST BOWL
WITH AVOCADO, HUMMUS AND BREAD ROLLS

INGREDIENTS

FOR THE BREAD ROLLS

1 avocado

½ cucumber

2 radishes

2 spring onions

2 tsp avocado oil

2 bread rolls (e.g. wholemeal or lye rolls)

EXTRAS

1 batch hummus (see page 20)

1 tsp sesame seeds

Fresh herbs

METHOD

1 Make the hummus as described on page 20. Halve the avocado, remove the stone and scoop out the flesh. Trim, wash and finely slice the cucumber, radishes and spring onions. Cut 2 cucumber slices into very thin strips as a garnish. Then divide the cucumber slices and two-thirds of the spring onions into two bowls and add an avocado half to each. Pour a little avocado oil into the middle of each avocado half.

2 Halve the bread rolls, spread each half with hummus, cover with radish slices and garnish with the cucumber strips and remaining spring onions. Finally, top with a sprinkling of sesame seeds and fresh herbs.

 TIP

You can replace the hummus with a batch of oriental dip (see recipe on page 22).

10 MINUTES

SEMOLINA PUDDING BOWL
WITH STEWED PLUMS

INGREDIENTS

FOR THE SEMOLINA PUDDING

400 ml almond milk

1 tbsp maple syrup

100 g white polenta or
  spelt semolina

250 g vegan yoghurt
  alternative (e.g. coconut,
  almond, soya)

FOR THE STEWED PLUMS

10 plums

1 lemon

¼ tsp ground cinnamon

1–2 tbsp maple syrup

EXTRAS

2 sprigs thyme

1 handful blackberries

Maple syrup

METHOD

1 Combine the almond milk and maple syrup in a small saucepan. Stir in the polenta or semolina and bring to the boil. Immediately lower the heat and simmer for 15 minutes, stirring constantly. Stir in a little more almond milk if necessary. Finally, add the yoghurt alternative and incorporate.

2 Wash, halve and de-stone the plums. Squeeze the lemon. In another saucepan, combine the plums, lemon juice, cinnamon and maple syrup with 50 ml of water and bring to the boil. Reduce the heat to low and simmer for 10 minutes. Add a little more water if necessary.

3 Wash the thyme and shake dry. Sort and wash the blackberries and carefully pat them dry. Then divide the semolina pudding into two bowls and garnish with stewed plums, blackberries and a sprig of thyme. Finally, drizzle with a little maple syrup and serve.

 TIP

If plums are unavailable, you can stew three apples instead. For a special touch, you can also add roasted nuts and seeds seasoned with a pinch of ground cinnamon.

25 MINUTES

MATCHA PUDDING BOWL

INGREDIENTS

FOR THE PUDDING

350 ml almond milk

½ tsp matcha powder

2 tbsp maple syrup

4 tbsp chia seeds

EXTRAS

1 kiwi fruit

4 tbsp coconut yoghurt
   alternative

2 tsp maple syrup

2 tsp ground almonds

2 tsp hemp seeds

4 small mint leaves

METHOD

1 Warm the almond milk in a small saucepan over a medium heat. Then pour the warm almond milk into a bowl, add the matcha powder through a small sieve and stir to dissolve. Mix in the maple syrup and chia seeds and rest for 10–15 minutes, until the seeds swell.

2 In the meantime, peel and slice the kiwi fruit for the topping and wash the mint leaves. Divide the matcha pudding into two bowls and top with coconut yoghurt alternative, kiwi fruit slices, maple syrup, almonds, hemp seeds and mint leaves.

 TIP

As an alternative, you can replace the matcha powder with twice the amount of baking cocoa and the kiwi fruit with a banana. Just as delicious!

20 MINUTES + 15 MINUTES RESTING TIME

FANCY FRITTATA BOWL

INGREDIENTS

190 g chickpea flour

3 tsp chia seeds

½ tsp baking powder

1 tsp maple syrup

1 tbsp olive oil

½ tsp curry powder

½ tsp sweet paprika

¼ tsp garlic powder

Salt and pepper

4 spring onions

18 cherry tomatoes

2 handfuls basil leaves

EXTRAS

1 (23 x15-cm) ovenproof dish

1 handful baby spinach

2 tsp olive oil

Salt

METHOD

1 Preheat the oven to 180°C and line an ovenproof dish with baking parchment.

2 In a bowl, make a batter by mixing the chickpea flour, chia seeds, baking powder, maple syrup, olive oil, spices and a pinch each of salt and pepper with 400 ml of water. Rest the mixture for 7–10 minutes, until the seeds swell.

3 In the meantime, trim, wash and finely slice the spring onions. Remove the stems and wash the cherry tomatoes. Set 8 aside and halve the remainder. Wash the basil leaves and shake dry. Set half aside and tear up the remainder. Next, fold the vegetables into the batter. Pour the batter into the dish, spread evenly and bake for 30–40 minutes, until golden brown. Remove the frittata from the oven and leave to cool a little.

4 Sort the baby spinach leaves, wash and shake dry. Then divide the spinach and the remaining tomatoes and basil into two shallow bowls. Cut the frittata into two rectangles of the same size and place each one on the bed of vegetables. Finally, drizzle with a little olive oil and sprinkle with salt.

 TIP

You can mix things up here according to your mood: for instance, instead of making the frittata with tomatoes and basil, you can use mushrooms, olives, onion, spinach or sliced leek. You can serve it with either the baby spinach or with rocket and apple and mustard dressing (see recipe on page 25).

50 MINUTES

SCRAMBLED EGGS BOWL
WITH TOAST AND GUACAMOLE

INGREDIENTS

FOR THE SCRAMBLED EGGS

200 g tofu

2 spring onions

¼ bunch chives

½ tsp curry powder

½ tsp paprika

Salt

3 tbsp vegan yoghurt substitute (e.g. coconut, almond, soya)

1 tsp maple syrup

2 tbsp olive oil

2 tomatoes

2 slices bread

EXTRAS

3 tbsp guacamole (see page 20)

2 tbsp hummus (see page 20)

2 tsp black sesame seeds

METHOD

1 For the scrambled eggs, drain and cut the tofu into pieces and then crumble them with your hands. Trim, wash and finely slice the spring onions. Wash and chop the chives.

2 In a bowl, make the seasoning by mixing the curry powder, paprika powder, yoghurt alternative, maple syrup and a pinch of salt with 3 tablespoons of water. Then heat 1 tablespoon of olive oil in a frying pan and add the tofu, spring onion and the seasoning mixture, coating the tofu well in the seasoning. Sauté over a medium heat for 6–7 minutes, stirring from time to time. Finally, mix in about two-thirds of the chives and cook briefly.

3 Wash and halve the tomatoes. Heat the remaining olive oil in another frying pan and sauté the tomatoes on both sides over a medium heat for 3–4 minutes. Cut the bread slices in half and toast them in a toaster.

4 Make the guacamole and hummus as described on page 20. Divide the scrambled eggs, guacamole and toast into two bowls. Arrange the tomatoes in the centre of each, top with a little hummus and sprinkle over everything with black sesame seeds and the remaining chives.

 TIP

The Oriental dip (see recipe on page 22) goes perfectly with this dish and can be used instead of the hummus for a deliciously exotic touch.

20 MINUTES

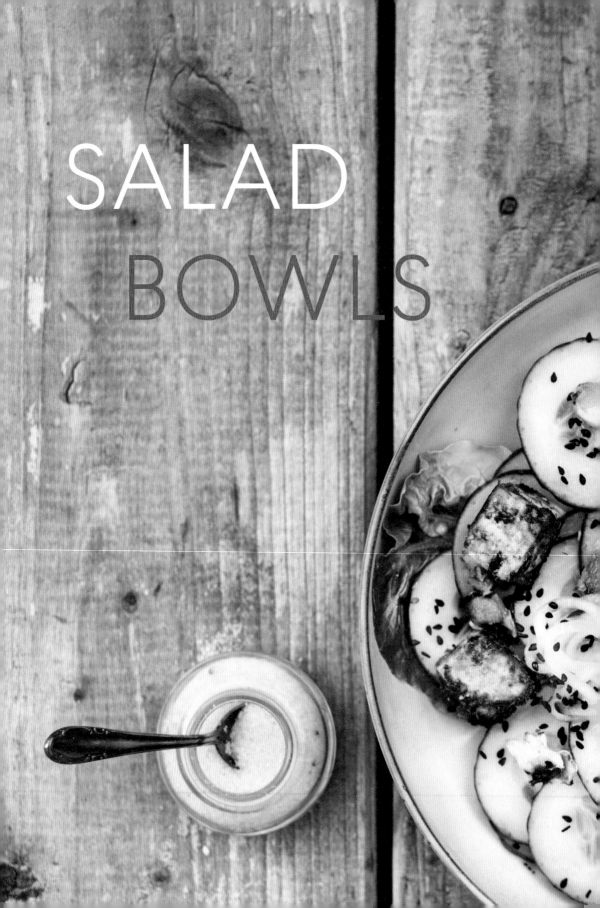

SALAD
BOWLS

SUPER SUMMER BOWL

INGREDIENTS

FOR THE SALAD

200 g rocket

½ cucumber

1 peach

50 g blueberries

50 g gooseberries

25 g almonds

2 tbsp white balsamic vinegar

2 tbsp olive oil

1 tsp maple syrup

Salt

EXTRAS

Fresh herbs (e.g. garden cress, parsley, basil)

METHOD

1 Wash, spin dry and tear up the rocket. Trim and wash the cucumber and thinly slice with a mandoline. Wash, halve and pit the peach. Cut into thin wedges. Sort the berries, wash and carefully pat dry. Then cut them in half. Coarsely chop the almonds.

2 To make the dressing, mix the balsamic vinegar with the olive oil, maple syrup, a pinch of salt and 3 tablespoons of water.

3 Wash the herbs, shake dry and pluck as many leaves from the stems as needed. Divide the rocket, cucumber slices, peach wedges and berries into two bowls. Top with the chopped almonds, drizzle with the dressing and sprinkle over with the herbs.

 TIP

The lemon and mint dressing (see recipe on page 25) also goes well with this colourful salad. Walnuts can be used instead of almonds in autumn to round out the flavour, while other seasonal fruits, such as strawberries in spring and pear wedges in autumn make excellent alternatives to the fruit used here.

15 MINUTES

FRUITY QUINOA BOWL
WITH FRESH PEACHES AND CARROTS

INGREDIENTS

FOR THE QUINOA AND
VEGETABLES

100 g tricolour quinoa

Salt

2 spring onions

2 carrots

1 peach

40 g almonds

¼ bunch parsley

20 g pumpkin seeds

EXTRAS

2 tbsp apple cider vinegar

2 tbsp olive oil

1 tsp maple syrup

1 tbsp medium-strength
   mustard

Salt

METHOD

1 Put the quinoa into a fine-mesh sieve and rinse under the tap until the water runs clear. Combine with 250 ml of salted water in a saucepan and briefly bring to the boil. Then lower the heat and simmer for another 20 minutes, stirring from time to time. Remove from the heat and keep warm.

2 In the meantime, trim, wash and finely slice the spring onions. Peel and cut the carrots into small dice. Wash, halve and pit the peach. Cut into thin wedges. Coarsely chop the almonds. Wash the parsley, shake dry and pluck the leaves from the stems.

3 Make a dressing by whisking the apple cider vinegar, olive oil, maple syrup, mustard and a pinch of salt with 3 tablespoons of water.

4 Divide the cooked quinoa, spring onions, diced carrots and peach wedges into two bowls and mix. Then sprinkle with the chopped almonds and pumpkin seeds and drizzle the dressing over everything.

 TIP

Instead of quinoa, you can also use other grains, such as bulgur or couscous. The fresh fruit can also be replaced by fruit in season, such as apples in spring and fresh figs in autumn, or of your preference.

30 MINUTES

SPICY ASIA BOWL
WITH KOHLRABI STRIPS AND MANGO

INGREDIENTS

FOR THE KOHLRABI

2 tbsp sesame seeds

1 pinch chilli flakes

2 kohlrabi

6 radishes

1 mango

½ bunch coriander

EXTRAS

1 clove garlic

1 small piece (about 1 cm)
  ginger

2 tsp sesame oil plus 1 tsp,
  for cooking

4 tbsp rice vinegar

1 tsp rice syrup

Salt and pepper

METHOD

1 Heat a dry frying pan over a medium heat and toast sesame seeds and chilli flakes for about 7 minutes, stirring constantly. Remove from the heat and leave to cool a little.

2 Clean and peel the kohlrabi and use a knife or mandoline to cut into 2-mm-thin strips. Trim and wash the radishes and finely slice with a mandoline. Peel the mango. Cut into the flesh on a diagonal and around the stone to separate the cheeks. Then cut the flesh into about 1-cm cubes. Wash the coriander, shake dry and pluck the leaves off the stems. Combine it with the kohlrabi, mango, radish, toasted sesame seeds and chilli flakes in a bowl and toss well.

3 To make the dressing, peel and finely chop the garlic and ginger. Heat the sesame oil in a frying pan and lightly brown the garlic and ginger. Then transfer both from the pan to a small bowl and mix with 2 tsp sesame oil, rice vinegar and rice syrup. Season with a little salt and pepper.

4 Divide the kohlrabi mixture into two bowls, drizzle with the dressing and serve.

 TIP

If you want turn the dish into a more substantial and filling main meal, add a serving of tofu fried with a tablespoon of soy sauce, a teaspoon of peanut oil and a teaspoon of maple syrup.

30 MINUTES

RED CHICORY BOWL
WITH FRESH FIGS AND ORANGES ON A BED OF MILLET

INGREDIENTS

FOR THE SALAD
80 g millet

Salt

3 heads red chicory

½ bunch fresh mint

2 oranges

2 fresh figs

Fresh cress (optional)

EXTRAS
1 orange

3 tbsp apple cider vinegar

2 tbsp olive oil

1 tbsp medium-strength mustard

Salt and pepper

METHOD

1 Put the millet into a fine-mesh sieve and rinse under the tap until the water runs clear. Then combine with about 350 ml of salted water in a saucepan and bring to the boil. Lower the heat and simmer for about 20 minutes, until all the liquid has been absorbed. Remove the pan from the heat and keep warm.

2 Wash and trim the chicory and shake the leaves dry. Wash the mint, shake dry and pluck the leaves from the stems. Peel the oranges, remove the pith and cut into pieces or slices. Wash and thinly slice the figs.

3 To make the dressing, squeeze the orange and whisk 2 tablespoons of the juice with the vinegar, oil, mustard, a pinch each of salt and pepper, and 2 tablespoons of water.

4 Divide the millet into two bowls and arrange the chicory leaves over it, followed by the orange pieces and figs. Scatter with the mint leaves and a little cress, if desired, and drizzle with the dressing.

 TIP

Fresh pineapple slices can also be used in place of the orange. The lemon and mint dressing (see recipe on page 25) makes an excellent accompaniment.

30 MINUTES

OUT-OF-THE-GARDEN BOWL

INGREDIENTS

FOR THE SALAD

100 g couscous

Salt

1 tin chickpeas (about 240 g drained weight)

10 radishes

¼ bunch fresh chives

3 tbsp apple cider vinegar

2 tbsp olive oil

1 tbsp medium-strength mustard

1 tsp maple syrup

Pepper

EXTRAS

2 tbsp pesto sauce

2 tsp black sesame seeds

METHOD

1 To prepare the couscous, bring 200 ml of salted water to the boil in a saucepan. Put the couscous into a heat-resistant bowl and pour in the boiling water. Allow the couscous to swell for 5–10 minutes and then keep warm.

2 Drain the chickpeas from the tin. Rinse, drain and put them into a bowl. Trim and wash the radishes and finely slice with a mandoline. Wash the chives, pat dry and finely chop with a sharp knife. To make the dressing, whisk the remaining ingredients together with a pinch each of salt and pepper, and 3 tablespoons of water.

3 Combine the couscous, chickpeas and radish slices in a large bowl, mix well and divide into two small bowls. Make small dots of pesto sauce over the salad and sprinkle with chives and black sesame seeds. Drizzle with the dressing before serving.

 TIP

You can replace the radishes with sliced carrots or cucumbers, and a handful of nuts roasted with salt and pepper to provide extra crunch.

20 MINUTES

LENTIL SALAD BOWL
WITH GOLDEN BEETROOT

INGREDIENTS

FOR THE SALAD

200 g cooked lentils
(from a tin)

½ courgette

1 tsp olive oil, for cooking

1 golden beetroot

1 yellow carrot

40 g sun-dried tomatoes
(in oil)

60 g lettuce (or other salad
leaves, e.g. lollo rossa or
mixed salad leaves)

Fresh herbs (e.g. garden cress)

4 edible flowers

2 tbsp sunflower seeds

FOR THE DRESSING

3 tbsp balsamic vinegar

2 tbsp olive oil

Salt and pepper

METHOD

1 To make the salad, drain the lentils from the tin. Rinse, drain and put them into a bowl. Trim, wash and finely slice the courgette.

2 Heat the oil in a frying pan and fry the courgette over a medium heat on both sides for 4–5 minutes, until golden brown.

3 Wash and slice the beetroot and the carrot into thin strips. Drain the sun-dried tomatoes of their oil and cut into quarters. Wash and sort the lettuce leaves, shake dry and coarsely tear. Wash the herbs, shake dry and pluck the leaves from the stems. Wash the flowers, shake dry and tear into pieces. Toss the vegetables with the lentils.

4 To make the dressing, whisk the vinegar and oil together with half a teaspoon of salt, a pinch of pepper, and 2 tablespoons of water.

5 Divide the lentil salad into two bowls and garnish with the sunflower seeds, flowers and fresh herbs. Drizzle with the dressing before serving.

 TIP

Add one batch of the oriental dip (see recipe on page 22) to give the dish an exotic twist.

30 MINUTES

WILD RICE SALAD BOWL

WITH COLOURFUL ROASTED VEGETABLES AND CHANTERELLES

INGREDIENTS

FOR THE SALAD

1 beetroot

1 golden beetroot

1 small parsnip

1 carrot

1 yellow carrot

1 red onion

2 tbsp olive oil

100 g wild rice

Salt

50 g chanterelle mushrooms

50 g red grapes

20 g hazelnuts

¼ bunch parsley

FOR THE DRESSING

2 tbsp apple cider vinegar

2 tbsp olive oil

1 tbsp medium-strength mustard

1 tsp maple syrup

1 pinch garlic powder

Salt and pepper

METHOD

1 Preheat the oven to 180°C and line a baking tray with baking parchment.

2 Trim, peel and cut both the red and golden beetroot into small pieces. Wash and thinly slice the parsnip and carrots. Peel and cut the onion into eighths. Arrange the vegetables on the tray, drizzle with 1 tablespoon of olive oil and roast in the oven for 20–25 minutes. Then take them out and leave to cool a little.

3 Put the wild rice into a fine-mesh sieve and rinse under the tap until the water runs clear. Combine with about 350 ml of salted water in a saucepan and bring to the boil. Then lower the heat and simmer for about 20 minutes, until all the liquid has been absorbed. Remove from the heat and keep warm.

4 Clean and halve the mushrooms. Heat a little oil in a frying pan and sauté the mushrooms for 4–5 minutes.

5 In the meantime, wash and halve the grapes. Coarsely chop the hazelnuts. Wash the parsley, shake dry and coarsely tear.

6 To make the dressing, whisk all the ingredients together with a pinch each of salt and pepper, and 2 tablespoons of water.

7 Combine the wild rice, roasted vegetables, mushrooms and grapes in a large bowl and toss well. Then divide into two smaller bowls, sprinkle with the chopped hazelnuts and parsley, and drizzle with the dressing.

30 MINUTES

20–25 MINUTES

CUCUMBER SALAD BOWL
WITH PEANUT TOFU CUBES AND FRIED GINGER

INGREDIENTS

FOR THE PEANUT TOFU
100 g firm tofu

1 tsp dried lemongrass

½ tsp garlic powder

1 pinch chilli flakes

1 tsp soy sauce

2 tsp peanut butter

2 tsp sesame oil, for cooking

FOR THE SALAD
1 (about 2-cm) length fresh
  ginger

2 tbsp olive oil, for cooking

2 cucumbers

6 large lettuce leaves

FOR THE DRESSING
2 tbsp rice vinegar

1 tsp rice syrup

1 tsp sesame oil

1 pinch garlic powder

Salt

EXTRAS
2 tsp black sesame seeds

METHOD

1 Drain and cut the tofu into cubes. For the marinade, combine the lemongrass, garlic powder, chilli flakes, soy sauce and peanut butter in a bowl. Mix the tofu into the marinade, coating well. Then heat the oil in a frying pan and fry the tofu over medium heat for 2–3 minutes, until crispy.

2 Peel and cut the ginger into thin slices with a knife or mandoline. Heat the olive oil in a small frying pan and fry the ginger slices over a high heat.

3 Trim and wash the cucumbers. For the garnish, cut roughly a third of one cucumber into thin strips with a mandoline or into noodles using a spiraliser. Thinly slice the remaining cucumbers with a knife or mandoline. Wash the parsley, shake dry and coarsely tear.

4 To make the dressing, whisk all ingredients together with a pinch of salt and 2 tablespoons of water.

5 Divide the salad into two shallow bowls and arrange the cucumber slices and fried tofu on top. Twist small bundles of cucumber strips or noodles with a fork and arrange over of the salad along with the fried ginger slices. Finally, sprinkle with black sesame seeds and drizzle with the dressing.

GREEK DOLMADES BOWL

INGREDIENTS

FOR THE SALAD

50 g pitted green olives

4 dolmades (ready-made)

100 g rocket

4 baby cucumbers
  (or ½ cucumber)

100 g multicoloured cherry
  tomatoes

1 small red onion

FOR THE DRESSING

1 lemon

4 tbsp olive oil

1 tsp maple syrup

Salt and pepper

EXTRAS

1 tsp sesame seeds

Watercress

METHOD

1 Drain the oil from the olives and the dolmades. Cut the dolmades in half.

2 Sort the rocket leaves, wash and shake dry. Trim and wash the baby cucumbers and thinly slice with a knife or mandoline. Wash and halve the cherry tomatoes. Peel, halve and cut the onion into strips.

3 For the dressing, whisk all the ingredients together with a pinch each of salt and pepper, and 2 tablespoons of water.

4 Divide the rocket into two bowls and arrange the olives, dolmades, tomatoes and onion over the top. Garnish with sesame seeds and cress. Drizzle with the dressing before serving.

 TIP

Serve with a batch of home-made hummus (see recipes on pages 20 and 21). You can also accompany this dish with fresh, crusty bread.

20 MINUTES

RAINBOW BOWL
WITH CASHEW DRESSING

INGREDIENTS

FOR THE SALAD

1 small sweet potato

½ lime

2 Cos (Romaine) lettuce
  hearts

1 tin kidney beans
  (about 240 g drained
  weight)

10 red and yellow
  cherry tomatoes

FOR THE LENTILS

50 g red lentils

½ onion – 1 clove garlic

½ tbsp olive oil

1 tbsp balsamic vinegar

1 tsp maple syrup

200 g chopped tomatoes
  (½ of a 400-g tin)

FOR THE DRESSING

2 limes

1 tbsp olive oil - 1 tsp cashew
  butter

1 tsp maple syrup

Salt and pepper

FOR THE TOPPING

4 tbsp cashew butter

30 g cashew nuts – 1 tbsp
  sesame seeds

METHOD

1 Clean, peel and cut the sweet potato into small cubes. In a saucepan, bring a sufficient amount of water to the boil and cook the sweet potato cubes for 15–20 minutes. Drain well and leave to cool a little.

2 In the meantime, put the lentils into a fine-mesh sieve and rinse under the tap until the water runs clear. Peel the onion and garlic, chop finely and heat together with the olive oil in a pan. After 2 minutes, deglaze the pan with the balsamic vinegar and add the maple syrup, 300 ml of water and the lentils. Mix and bring to the boil. Lower the heat and simmer for 12 minutes. Next, stir in the chopped tomatoes, raise the heat and bring back to the boil. Lower the heat again and simmer for 5 more minutes. Remove from heat and keep warm.

3 To make the dressing, squeeze the limes and whisk the juice together with the remaining ingredients, a pinch each of salt and pepper, and 2 tablespoons of water.

4 Cut the half lime into thin wedges. Separate the lettuce hearts, wash and shake dry the leaves. Set aside 6 medium leaves and cut the remainder into strips. Drain the beans from the tin. Rinse, drain and put them into a bowl. Wash and halve the cherry tomatoes.

5 Place 3 lettuce leaves in each bowl. Then arrange the remaining leaves and the kidney beans, lentils, tomatoes and sweet potatoes over them. Finally, garnish with lime wedges, cashew butter, cashews and sesame seeds. Drizzle with the dressing.

30 MINUTES

WEEKDAY
BOWLS

TAGLIATELLE BOWL
WITH LEMON, BASIL AND CHICKPEAS

INGREDIENTS

250 g tagliatelle

Salt

1 tin chickpeas
(about 240 g drained
weight)

100 g cherry tomatoes

2 cloves garlic

1 lemon

2 tbsp olive oil, for frying

1 tbsp maple syrup

Pepper

½ bunch basil

2 tsp sesame seeds

METHOD

1 In a saucepan, bring a sufficient amount of salted water to the boil and cook the pasta according to the instructions on the package.

2 In the meantime, drain the chickpeas from the tin, rinse and leave to drain. Trim and wash the cherry tomatoes. Peel and finely chop the garlic. Squeeze the lemon.

3 Heat the olive oil in a frying pan. Add the maple syrup, half a teaspoon of salt and a pinch of pepper. After about 30 seconds, deglaze the pan with the lemon juice. Then add 25 ml of water, the tomatoes and chickpeas, and sauté for about 10 minutes.

4 Transfer the pasta to a sieve or colander and drain well. Wash the basil, shake dry and pluck the leaves from the stems. Then add the pasta together with the basil leaves to the tomatoes and continue to sauté for 2 more minutes. Finally, adjust the seasoning with salt and pepper. Divide the tagliatelle and contents of the pan into two bowls, sprinkle with sesame seeds and serve.

 TIP

Sautéed courgette and mushrooms add variety. Simply wash and cut the vegetables into thin slices and sauté in a frying pan with a little oil.

30 MINUTES

JACKFRUIT NACHOS BOWL

INGREDIENTS

FOR THE SALSA

1 tin jackfruit (about 240 g drained weight)

1 tin kidney beans (about 255 g drained weight)

1 tin sweetcorn (about 285 g drained weight)

1 onion

1 clove of garlic

1 tbsp coconut oil

2 tsp sweet paprika

1 pinch chilli powder

25 ml espresso coffee

1 tsp maple syrup

400 g jar passata

Salt and pepper

EXTRAS

4 tbsp guacamole (see page 20)

1 lime

50 g spinach

½ bunch coriander

100 g tortilla chips

Sesame seeds

METHOD

1 Drain the jackfruit, beans and sweetcorn from their tins, rinse and leave to drain. Peel and finely chop the onion and garlic. Heat the coconut oil in a saucepan. Add the paprika and chilli, toast for about 2 minutes and then deglaze the pan with the coffee and 50 ml of water. Add maple syrup, onion and garlic, and sauté for about 3 minutes, stirring constantly, until golden. Then add the passata, jackfruit, kidney beans and sweetcorn, season with a pinch each of salt and pepper, and bring to a boil. Lower the heat and simmer for 10 minutes, stirring often.

2 In the meantime, make the guacamole as described on page 20. Cut the lime into quarters. Wash the spinach and shake dry. Wash the coriander, shake dry and pluck the leaves from the stems.

3 Divide the guacamole, spinach and tortilla chips into two bowls. Top each bowl with 2 tablespoons of guacamole and a quarter lime, and sprinkle with coriander leaves and sesame seeds.

30 MINUTES

QUINOA AND CARROT BOWL

WITH ALMOND AND SESAME GRANOLA

INGREDIENTS

100 g tricolour quinoa

Salt

2 oranges

3 carrots

30 g almonds

1 small onion

2 cloves garlic

½ broccoli head

1 tbsp olive oil, for frying

1 tbsp sesame seeds

1 tsp maple syrup

2 tbsp dried cranberries

METHOD

1 Put the quinoa into a fine-mesh sieve and rinse under the tap until the water runs clear. Then combine with about 400 ml of salted water in a saucepan and bring to the boil. Lower the heat and simmer for 20 minutes, until all liquid has been absorbed. Then remove from heat and keep warm.

2 Squeeze one orange and set aside the juice. Halve and slice the other orange. Peel, trim and cut the carrots into thin strips. Coarsely chop the almonds. Peel and finely chop the onion and garlic. Trim, wash and divide the broccoli into florets. Combine in a saucepan with the carrots and add water. Bring to the boil, lower the heat and cook for 3–4 minutes. Then drain in a sieve or colander.

3 Heat the olive oil in a frying pan. Add the onion, garlic, sesame seeds, maple syrup and half a teaspoon of salt, and sauté over a high heat. After about 30 seconds, deglaze the pan with the orange juice, lower the heat and add the broccoli, carrots and orange slices. Sauté for 5–6 more minutes. Shortly before finishing, add the dried cranberries and sauté together.

4 Divide the quinoa into two bowls and top with the sautéed vegetables.

 TIP

The quinoa can easily be replaced by wild rice. Its nutty flavour goes wonderfully with this bowl. The creamy nut dressing on page 25 perfectly complements the earthy flavours of this bowl.

30 MINUTES

EAT YOUR GREENS BOWL

INGREDIENTS

100 g millet

Salt

1 broccoli head

100 g frozen peas

1 small chilli pepper

Watercress

100 g vegan yoghurt substitute (e.g. coconut, almond, soya)

1 tbsp sesame butter (tahini)

1 tsp lemon juice

Salt and pepper

EXTRAS
1 tbsp sesame seeds

METHOD

1 Put the millet into a fine-mesh sieve and rinse under the tap until the water runs clear. Combine with about 400 ml of salted water in a saucepan and bring to the boil. Lower the heat and simmer for about 20 minutes, until all liquid has been absorbed. Then remove from heat and keep warm.

2 In the meantime, trim, wash and divide the broccoli into florets. Combine in a saucepan with the peas and add water. Bring to the boil and lower the heat. Cook for 5–7 minutes and then drain.

3 Wash and very finely slice the chilli pepper. Wash the watercress and shake dry.

4 To make the dressing, mix all remaining ingredients and season with a pinch each of salt and pepper. Divide the millet, broccoli and peas into two shallow bowls. Place 1 tablespoon of dressing in the middle of each bowl and sprinkle over everything with chilli, watercress and sesame seeds.

 TIP

A handful of fresh sprouts not only add extra nutrients to this bowl but also rounds it off perfectly.

30 MINUTES

CHANTERELLE AND COURGETTE BOWL

INGREDIENTS

120 g millet

½ red onion

1 tbsp olive oil, for cooking

1 tbsp white balsamic vinegar

1 tsp maple syrup

150 ml vegetable stock

½ courgette

40 g chanterelle mushrooms

6 sun-dried tomatoes (in oil)

Salt and pepper

8 basil leaves

Garden cress

METHOD

1 Put the millet into a fine-mesh sieve and rinse under the tap until the water runs clear.

2 Peel and finely chop the onion. In a small saucepan, heat the olive oil and sauté the onion until translucent. After about 2 minutes, deglaze the pan with the balsamic vinegar and stir in the maple syrup, vegetable stock, millet and 150 ml of water. Bring to the boil. Then lower the heat and simmer for 10 minutes, stirring from time to time.

3 In the meantime, trim and wash the courgette. Cut it into quarters lengthways and then into slices. Clean the mushrooms. Drain some of the oil from the sun-dried tomatoes and cut them into quarters.

4 Add the courgette, mushrooms and sun-dried tomatoes to the millet and season with a pinch each of salt and pepper. Wash the garden cress and shake dry. Divide the millet and vegetables into two bowls and garnish with the basil leaves and some garden cress.

 TIP

The millet can be replaced with rice or quinoa, according to preference. And for an extra bit of crunch, add a handful of chopped roasted nuts with a spicy seasoning.

🕐 30 MINUTES

MEXICAN RICE BOWL

INGREDIENTS

1 small sweet potato

100 g frozen green beans

1 tin kidney beans
(about 240 g drained
weight)

100 g rice

1 lime

1 small onion

1 clove garlic

1 tbsp coconut oil

1 tsp sweet paprika

1 pinch chilli flakes

½ tsp salt

1 tbsp maple syrup

200 ml coconut milk

4 tbsp passata

3 tbsp peanut butter

EXTRAS

1 handful spinach

1 lime

METHOD

1 Clean, peel and cut the sweet potato into small cubes. In a saucepan, bring a sufficient amount of water to the boil and cook the sweet potato cubes for 15–20 minutes. After about 10 minutes, add the green beans and cook for the remaining time. Pour the contents of the pan into a sieve or colander and drain well.

2 Drain the beans from the tin, rinse and leave to drain. Put the rice into a fine-mesh sieve and rinse under the tap until the water runs clear.

3 Squeeze the lime. Peel and finely chop the onion and garlic. In a saucepan, heat the coconut oil and toast the spices with maple syrup over a medium heat for about 30 seconds. Then deglaze the pan with the lime juice. In another saucepan, mix the rice with 200 ml of water, the coconut milk, passata and peanut butter, and bring to the boil. Then lower the heat and simmer for 20–25 minutes, stirring from time to time. Shortly before the end of the cooking time, stir in the sweet potato cubes and green beans.

4 Sort the spinach leaves, wash and shake dry. Halve the lime, then cut each half into quarters. Divide the rice with vegetables into two bowls and top with the spinach and lime wedges.

 TIP

A small pumpkin or winter squash can be used instead of the sweet potato.

30 MINUTES

HOT CREAMY SOUP BOWL
WITH SWEET POTATOES AND CARROTS

INGREDIENTS

FOR THE SOUP

500 g sweet potatoes

2 yellow carrots

1 clove garlic

3 tbsp olive oil

1 tsp chilli flakes

½ tsp ground ginger

¼ tsp ground coriander

1 tsp salt

1 tbsp white balsamic vinegar

EXTRAS

50 g quinoa

Salt

½ red onion

1 handful lamb's lettuce

METHOD

1 Preheat the oven to 180°C and line a baking tray with baking parchment.

2 Clean, peel and cut the sweet potatoes into small cubes. Wash, peel and cut the carrots into about 1-cm-thick slices. Place the cut vegetables in the baking tray and roast in the hot oven (middle shelf) for about 20 minutes.

3 In the meantime, put the quinoa into a fine-mesh sieve and rinse under the tap until the water runs clear. Combine with about 150 ml of salted water in a saucepan and bring to the boil. Lower the heat and simmer for about 20 minutes, until all liquid has been absorbed. Then remove from heat and keep warm.

4 In the meantime, wash and halve the garlic clove. Heat the olive oil in a saucepan, add the spices together with the salt and toast them for about 1 minute. Deglaze the pan with balsamic vinegar, add the garlic and 100 ml of water, and cook over a low heat for 2–3 minutes. Then add the sweet potatoes, carrots and 300 ml of water, and bring back to the boil. Lower the heat and blend the mixture to a creamy consistency with a hand-held blender.

5 Peel and slice the onion into rings. Wash the lamb's lettuce and shake dry.

6 Just before serving, bring the soup back to the boil and then divide it into two bowls. Garnish each bowl with 2 tablespoons of quinoa, a few onion rings and some lamb's lettuce.

30 MINUTES

20 MINUTES

BELLA ITALIA BOWL
WITH LENTIL RAGU

INGREDIENTS

FOR THE LENTIL RAGU
100 g red lentils

½ onion

2 cloves garlic

1 tbsp olive oil

2 tbsp balsamic vinegar

1 tsp maple syrup

10 cherry tomatoes

400 g tin chopped tomatoes

EXTRAS
140 g fusilli

¼ bunch basil

2 tbsp grated almonds

2 tbsp olive oil

Salt

METHOD

1 In a saucepan, bring a sufficient amount of salted water to the boil and cook the pasta according to the instructions on the package.

2 In the meantime, make the lentil ragu. Put the lentils into a fine-mesh sieve and rinse under the tap until the water runs clear. Peel and finely chop the onions and garlic. Heat the olive oil in a saucepan and sauté the onion and garlic. After 2 minutes, deglaze the pan with the balsamic vinegar. Then add the maple syrup, lentils and 300 ml of water. Mix and bring to the boil. Lower the heat and simmer for about 12 minutes.

3 In the meantime, wash the basil, shake dry and pluck the leaves from the stems. Wash and halve the cherry tomatoes.

4 Next, add the chopped tomatoes to the lentils and bring back to the boil. Lower the heat again, add the cherry tomato halves and simmer for 5 more minutes. Transfer the pasta to a sieve or colander and drain well.

5 Divide the pasta into two shallow bowls and cover with lentil ragu. Sprinkle with the basil leaves and grated almonds, drizzle with a little olive oil and serve.

25 MINUTES

EASY PASTA BOWL
WITH PEPPER AND ALMOND SAUCE

INGREDIENTS

FOR THE SAUCE

1 lemon

2 jars roasted red peppers
    in brine (220 g drained
    weight, each)

50 g blanched almonds

2 tbsp olive oil

2 tsp maple syrup

¼ tsp salt

Pepper

EXTRAS

160 g pasta (e.g. penne)

Salt

2–3 sprigs thyme

2 tbsp ground almonds

METHOD

1   In a saucepan, bring a sufficient amount of salted water to
    the boil and cook the pasta according to the instructions
    on the package.

2   Squeeze the lemon. Drain the peppers from the jar, rinse
    and leave to drain. Combine the peppers with lemon juice,
    almonds, oil, maple syrup, salt, a pinch of pepper and
    2 tablespoons of water, and blend until creamy in a
    blender or with a hand-held blender.

3   Wash the thyme, shake dry and coarsely tear. Drain the
    pasta well and divide into two bowls. Spread the sauce
    over the top, garnish with the thyme and sprinkle with
    the ground almonds.

 TIP

For a quick home-made tomato sauce, replace the grilled
peppers with sun-dried tomatoes preserved in oil. Roasted
sunflower seeds can be used instead of almonds. Roast the
seeds yourself in a dry frying pan over a medium heat for
4–5 minutes.

25 MINUTES

ONE-POT BUCKWHEAT BOWL

WITH PEAS AND MANGETOUT

INGREDIENTS

120 g buckwheat

1 small onion

1 clove garlic

1 tbsp olive oil

½ tsp curry powder

½ tsp ground coriander

¼ tsp ground cumin

¼ tsp ground ginger

1 tsp coconut blossom sugar

Salt

25 ml vegan white wine (or
    25 ml apple cider vinegar)

200 g frozen peas

150 g frozen mangetout

1 spring onion

1 tsp hemp seeds

METHOD

1 Put the buckwheat into a fine-mesh sieve and rinse under the tap until the water runs clear.

2 Peel and finely chop the onion and garlic. Combine in a saucepan with the olive oil, spices, sugar and a pinch of salt, and sauté over a medium heat for about 30 seconds. Deglaze the pan with the white wine and simmer for 2 minutes. Add the buckwheat and 400–500 ml of water, stir well and bring back to the boil. Then lower the heat to medium and cook for 20–25 minutes, stirring from time to time.

3 In the meantime, fill a saucepan with sufficient water, bring to the boil and blanch the peas and mangetout. Set aside. Trim, wash and finely slice the spring onion.

4 Shortly before the buckwheat finishes cooking, carefully mix in the blanched peas and mangetout, and leave to finish. Then divide the buckwheat with vegetables into two bowls, sprinkle with the spring onion and hemp seeds, and serve.

🕐 25 MINUTES

CRÊPE BOWL
WITH A PUMPKIN SEED CREAM FILLING

INGREDIENTS

FOR THE CRÊPES

2 tbsp chia seeds

50 g spelt flour

40 g chickpea flour

½ tsp baking powder

1 tbsp black sesame seeds

1 tbsp linseed oil

170 ml almond milk

1 tbsp coconut oil, for
   cooking

FOR THE PUMPKIN SEED CREAM FILLING

75 g vegan quark alternative

30 g ground pumpkin seeds

1 tbsp linseed oil

1 tsp maple syrup

Salt

EXTRAS

150 g cherry tomatoes

½ lemon

1 tbsp olive oil

1 tsp maple syrup

Salt

6 lettuce leaves

1 tbsp pumpkin seeds

METHOD

1 Put the chia seeds in a bowl with 50 ml of water, mix well and leave to swell for about 15 minutes.

2 In the meantime, make the filling. Mix the ingredients together with a tablespoon of water, season with a little salt and refrigerate until ready to use.

3 Wash the cherry tomatoes Squeeze the lemon. Heat the olive oil in a frying pan and sauté the tomatoes with maple syrup, lemon juice and a pinch of salt over a low heat for 10–12 minutes.

4 To make the crêpes, combine both flours with the baking powder, sesame seeds, linseed oil, almond milk and chia seeds and mix to a smooth batter.

5 Melt the coconut oil in a frying pan and swirl the pan to coat evenly. Use a ladle (equivalent to 5 tablespoons) to pour crêpe batter into the pan. Gently swirl the pan to spread the batter evenly over the bottom. Cook the crêpes over a medium heat for 2–3 minutes each side, until golden brown. Repeat the process for the remaining batter.

6 Place the finished crêpes on a plate and spread them with filling. Roll them up and cut into about 2-cm lengths.

7 Wash the lettuce leaves, shake dry and coarsely tear. Divide them into two bowls. Arrange the crêpe rolls and tomatoes on top and sprinkle with the pumpkin seeds.

 TIP

Serve with a green salad dressed with the balsamic vinegar dressing (see recipe on page 24).

40 MINUTES

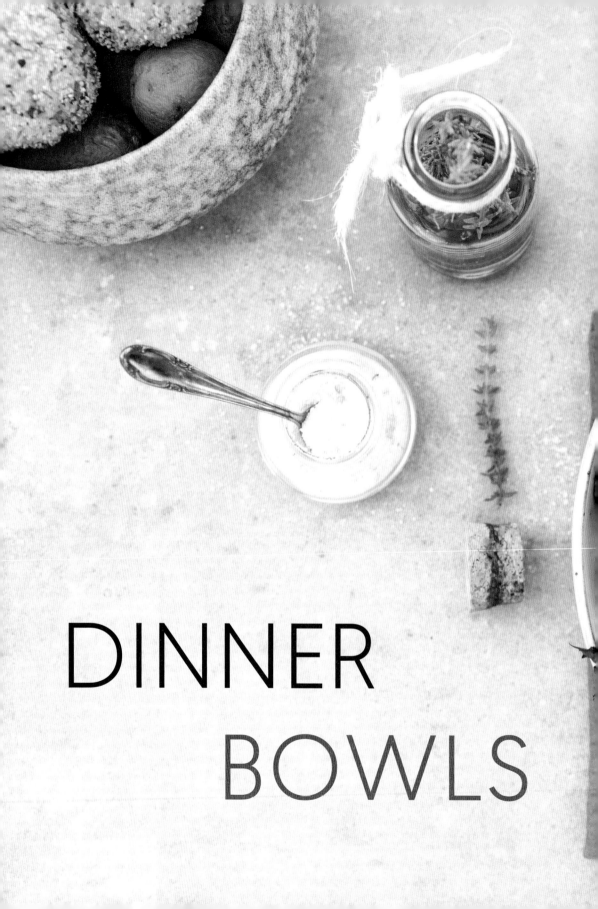

DINNER
BOWLS

BEAN AND COCOA BOWL
WITH COUSCOUS

INGREDIENTS

FOR THE BEANS

1 red onion

2 cloves garlic

3 carrots

1 yellow pepper

1 lemon

2 tbsp coconut oil

¼ tsp chilli flakes

1 tsp caraway seeds

1 tbsp sweet paprika

Salt and pepper

1 tsp dried oregano

400 g jar passata

1 tsp maple syrup

1 tbsp baking cocoa

1 tin haricot beans
   (about 240 g drained
   weight)

EXTRAS

100 g couscous

Salt

¼ bunch parsley

2 tbsp sesame seeds

METHOD

1   Peel and finely chop the onion and garlic. Trim and peel the carrots. Halve, trim and wash the pepper. Cut the carrots and pepper into small dice. Squeeze the lemon.

2   Heat the coconut oil in a saucepan. Add the spices, salt, pepper and oregano and toast them for about 2 minutes. Then deglaze the pan with lemon juice and 50 ml of water. Add the passata, maple syrup, baking cocoa and vegetables, and bring the sauce to the boil.

3   In the meantime, drain the beans from the tin. Rinse, drain and add them to the sauce. Simmer for 10 minutes.

4   For the couscous, bring 200 ml of salted water to the boil in a saucepan. Put the couscous into a heat-resistant bowl and pour in the boiling water. Allow the couscous to swell for 5–10 minutes.

5   Wash the parsley, shake dry and pluck the leaves from the stems. Divide the couscous into two shallow bowls, top with the bean and cocoa stew, and garnish with parsley and sesame seeds.

 TIP

The couscous can be replaced with a gluten-free alternative, such as quinoa, and the carrots can be replaced by a quarter of an uchiki (red) kuri squash in autumn.

40 MINUTES

THE THOUSAND AND ONE NIGHTS BOWL

INGREDIENTS

FOR THE TABBOULEH

100 g couscous

Salt

1 red onion

2 tomatoes

½ cucumber

½ bunch parsley

1 lemon – 2 tbsp olive oil

1 tsp maple syrup

FOR THE TOFU

3 tbsp ground coriander

1 tbsp sweet paprika

1 tbsp cumin seeds

½ tsp each of ground turmeric, cinnamon and cardamom

1 tbsp ground ginger

1 pinch chilli flakes

2 tbsp olive oil

1 tsp maple syrup

Salt and pepper

200 g firm tofu

1 tin chickpeas (about 240 g drained weight)

Rapeseed oil

EXTRAS

Plain hummus (see page 20)

2 tbsp sesame seeds

1 pinch chilli flakes

METHOD

1 For the tabbouleh, bring 200 ml salted water to a boil. Put the couscous into a heat-resistant bowl and pour in the boiling water. Allow the couscous to swell for 5–10 minutes. Peel and finely chop the onion. Wash and cut the tomatoes into small dice. Clean, wash and cut the cucumber into small dice. Wash the parsley, shake dry and pluck the leaves from the stems. Add all the vegetables to the couscous and carefully fold in. Squeeze the lemon and combine the juice with olive oil and maple syrup. Season with salt, mix and pour the dressing over the tabbouleh.

2 To make the tofu marinade, mix the spices with the olive oil, maple syrup, a pinch each of salt and pepper, and 2 tablespoons of water. Cut the tofu into cubes. Drain the chickpeas from the tin, rinse and leave to drain. Put the tofu cubes and chickpeas into separate bowls and pour over the marinade.

3 Heat a little oil in a frying pan and fry the marinated tofu cubes on all sides over a medium heat. Take out the tofu and wipe the pan clean. Then heat a little more oil and fry the marinated chickpeas until crispy.

4 Divide the tabbouleh, tofu cubes and chickpeas into two shallow bowls. Put 2 tablespoons of hummus in the centre of each and sprinkle everything with sesame seeds and chilli flakes.

 TIP

For added variety, try this dish with the curried sweet potato hummus shown on page 21 instead of the plain version.

30 MINUTES

ORIENTAL CURRY BOWL

INGREDIENTS

FOR THE CURRIED RICE

100 g rice – salt

½ red onion

1 tbsp coconut oil

1 tsp curry powder

½ tsp ground coriander

¼ tsp ground cumin

1 lemon – 25 g raisins

FOR THE SALAD

½ red onion – 3 baby
cucumbers

100 g multicoloured cherry
tomatoes

½ bunch parsley – 2 tbsp
wine vinegar

2 tbsp olive oil – 1 tsp mustard

1 tsp maple syrup – salt –
pepper

FOR THE TOFU SKEWERS

½ tsp salt – ¼ tsp garlic
powder

½ tsp sweet paprika

¼ tsp ground cumin

Pepper – ¼ tsp each of
ground turmeric, coriander
and ginger

Chilli powder – 1 tsp maple
syrup

100 g firm tofu

1 tin chickpeas (about 240 g
drained weight) – rapeseed
oil

EXTRAS

Yoghurt dip (see page 22)

1 tbsp sesame seeds – salt –
chilli powder

METHOD

1 Put the rice into a fine-mesh sieve and rinse under the tap until the water runs clear. Peel and finely dice the onion. Heat the coconut oil in a saucepan and toast the spices with a quarter teaspoon of salt over a medium heat for about 30 seconds. Squeeze the lemon and add the juice to the pan. Add the onion and 50 ml of water, and sauté for 3–4 minutes. Then add the rice, raisins and pour in about 250 ml of salted water and bring to the boil. Lower the heat and simmer for about 20 minutes, stirring from time to time, until all the liquid has been absorbed. Remove from the heat and keep warm.

2 To make the salad, peel, quarter and finely slice the onion. Trim, wash and thinly slice the cucumbers. Wash and halve the cherry tomatoes. Wash the parsley, shake dry and tear into small pieces. In a bowl, toss the lettuce with the onion, cucumber, tomatoes and parsley. To make the dressing, mix all the remaining ingredients and season with a pinch each of salt and pepper. Add the dressing to the salad and toss well.

3 To prepare the tofu, mix the spices with the maple syrup and 2 tablespoons of water. Cut the tofu into cubes. Drain the chickpeas from the tin, rinse and leave to drain. Put the tofu cubes and chickpeas into separate bowls and marinate with spice mixture. Thread the marinated tofu cubes onto bamboo skewers.

4 Heat a little rapeseed oil in a frying pan. Fry the tofu skewers over a medium heat until golden brown all over. Take out the tofu skewers and wipe the pan clean. Then heat a little more oil and fry the marinated chickpeas until crispy.

5 Divide the curried rice, chickpeas and salad into two shallow bowls. Arrange one tofu skewer and a tablespoon of dip over the contents of the bowl and sprinkle with sesame seeds, salt and chilli powder.

CASHEW AND POLENTA BOWL
WITH SPICY VEGETABLES

INGREDIENTS

FOR THE POLENTA

500 ml almond milk

120 g fine cornmeal

2 tsp coconut oil

Ayurveda rock salt (or plain salt) and pepper

100 g cashew cheese

FOR THE VEGETABLES

1 tbsp sweet paprika

1 pinch chilli powder

¼ tsp ground cumin

2 tablespoons olive oil, a little for cooking

1 tsp maple syrup

Salt

4 small carrots

1 small yellow courgette

10 cherry tomatoes

½ red onion

10 pitted olives

EXTRAS

Garden cress

METHOD

1 To make the polenta, put the almond milk into a saucepan and bring to the boil. Stir in the cornmeal, then add the coconut oil and a pinch each of salt and pepper. Reduce the heat to low and leave to swell for about 15 minutes. In the meantime, cut the cashew cheese into small cubes. About 5 minutes before the polenta finishes cooking, stir in the cashew cheese. If the polenta thickens too much, add a little more almond milk. Remove from the heat and keep warm.

2 To prepare the vegetables, whisk together the paprika, chilli powder, ground cumin, oil, maple syrup and a pinch of salt in a small bowl. Trim, peel and thinly slice the carrots and courgette. Wash and halve the cherry tomatoes. Peel and slice the onion into thin rings. Combine the vegetables in a bowl and mix with the seasoned oil to marinate.

3 Heat a little olive oil in a frying pan and sauté the marinated vegetables over a medium heat for about 10 minutes. Add a little more water if necessary so that there is liquid in the pan.

4 Divide the polenta into two bowls, top with the sautéed vegetables and the olives. Sprinkle with some fresh garden cress and serve.

35 MINUTES

CAULIFLOWER BALL BOWL
WITH ROASTED POTATOES

INGREDIENTS

FOR THE CAULIFLOWER BALLS

3 tbsp chia seeds

250 g small potatoes

500 g cauliflower

1 red onion

3 cloves garlic

80 g cornmeal, plus a little more for dredging

1 tsp maple syrup

Juice of ½ lemon

1 tsp salt and pepper

FOR THE SALAD

100 g mixed salad leaves

1 yellow carrot

2 tbsp balsamic vinegar

2 tbsp olive oil – 1 tsp maple syrup

Fresh herbs – salt

EXTRAS

1 small courgette

Olive oil, for cooking

2 tbsp yoghurt dip (see page 22)

6 edible flowers

Garden cress

METHOD

1 Combine the chia seeds with 50 ml of water and leave to swell for about 15 minutes. Preheat the oven to 180°C and line a baking tray with baking parchment. Brush and then wash the potatoes and place them on a baking tray.

2 Trim, wash and finely grate the cauliflower. Peel and finely chop the onion and garlic. Combine in a bowl with the swollen chia seeds and the remaining ingredients. Season with a pinch of pepper and mix well. If the mixture is too wet, add a little more cornmeal. Then use your hands to shape the mixture into balls of about 5 cm in size. Put a little cornmeal in a shallow bowl and dredge the cauliflower balls. Place the balls on the baking tray with the potatoes and bake in the hot oven (middle shelf) for 30–40 minutes, until golden brown. Remove from the oven and leave to cool a little.

3 Trim, wash and thinly slice the courgette. Heat a little oil in a frying pan and fry the courgette slices on both sides over a medium heat for 4–5 minutes. Then wipe the pan clean and heat a little more oil. Cut the cooled potatoes in half and fry them for 6–7 minutes until crispy.

4 Wash and sort the lettuce leaves, shake dry and coarsely tear. Trim, peel and finely slice the carrot. Mix the salad leaves with the carrot slices in a bowl. Mix all the remaining ingredients together to make the dressing. Add the dressing to the salad and toss well.

5 Make the yoghurt dip as described on page 22. Divide the salad, roasted potatoes, courgette and cauliflower balls into two shallow bowls and garnish each bowl with a tablespoon of dip, the flowers and garden cress. Season with a little salt and pepper.

55 MINUTES

FENNEL DAL BOWL

INGREDIENTS

FOR THE DAL

1 (about 2-cm) length fresh
    ginger

½ red onion

3 cloves garlic

1 lemon

1 tbsp coconut oil

2 tsp curry powder

1 tsp cumin seeds

1 tsp ground coriander

1 tsp maple syrup

160 g yellow split lentils

Salt and pepper

EXTRAS

100 g red quinoa

1 sweet potato

1 fennel bulb

Olive oil, for cooking

1 tbsp black sesame seeds

1 tsp maple syrup

½ tsp salt

½ onion

1 handful salad leaves
    (e.g. lamb's lettuce)

METHOD

1 Peel and finely chop the ginger, onion and garlic. Squeeze the lemon. Heat the coconut oil in a saucepan and toast the spices for about 2 minutes. Then deglaze the pan with the lemon juice and 50 ml of water. Add the maple syrup, onion and garlic, and sauté for about 3 minutes, stirring constantly. Stir in 500–600 ml of water and bring to the boil. Reduce the heat to low, add the lentils and simmer for 20–25 minutes, stirring from time to time, until all the liquid is absorbed. Season with salt and pepper.

2 In the meantime, put the quinoa into a fine-mesh sieve and rinse under the tap until the water runs clear. Then combine with 300 ml of water in a saucepan and bring to the boil. Reduce heat to medium and simmer for about 20 minutes, stirring from time to time. Leave to cool a little.

3 In the meantime, brush, peel and cut the sweet potato into bite-sized cubes. Trim, wash and slice the fennel. Put the vegetables into a saucepan with sufficient water and bring to the boil. Then lower the heat, cook the vegetables for 14–16 minutes and drain. Heat a little oil in a frying pan and stir in the sesame seeds, maple syrup and salt. Add the vegetables, coat well and lightly sauté.

4 Peel and slice the onion into thin rings. Sort the salad leaves, wash and shake dry.

5 Divide the sweet potatoes, fennel, dal and quinoa into two shallow bowls. Serve topped with onion rings, salad leaves and sesame seeds.

40 MINUTES

ROASTED SQUASH BOWL
WITH RED CABBAGE AND QUINOA AND BEAN SALAD

INGREDIENTS

FOR THE RED CABBAGE
½ red cabbage

Olive oil, for cooking

2 tbsp white balsamic vinegar

Salt and pepper

FOR THE SALAD
100 g red quinoa

Salt

400 g tin haricot beans
  (about 240 g drained
  weight)

½ bunch chives

FOR THE DRESSING
2 tbsp apple cider vinegar

2 tbsp olive oil

1 tsp maple syrup

Salt and pepper

EXTRAS
½ (about 250 g) uchiki (red)
  kuri squash

Salt and pepper

METHOD

1 Put the quinoa into a fine-mesh sieve and rinse under the tap until the water runs clear. Combine with about 250 ml of salted water in a saucepan and briefly bring to the boil. Then lower the heat and simmer for 20 minutes, stirring from time to time. Remove from the heat and keep warm.

2 Preheat the oven to 180°C and line a baking tray with baking parchment.

3 Trim and halve the squash, remove the seeds and cut the flesh into wedges. Place the squash wedges on the baking tray and roast in the oven (middle shelf) for about 20 minutes.

4 Trim and wash the cabbage, halve and cut into fine strips with a mandoline. Heat a little oil in a frying pan and sauté the cabbage for about 3 minutes over a medium heat. Deglaze the pan with the balsamic vinegar and continue to sauté for 2–3 more minutes. Season with salt and pepper.

5 To make the dressing, mix the ingredients with 2 tablespoons of water. Make the bean salad by draining the beans from the tin. Rinse and leave to drain. Wash the chives, shake dry and finely chop. Add the beans and about two-thirds of the chopped chives to the quinoa. Drizzle with the dressing and mix well.

6 Divide the quinoa and bean salad, red cabbage and squash wedges into two shallow bowls. Season with salt and pepper, and sprinkle with sesame seeds.

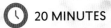 20 MINUTES

 20 MINUTES

ROASTED VEGETABLE BOWL

WITH POTATO AND ALMOND SOUP

INGREDIENTS

FOR THE SOUP

50 g blanched almonds

500 g waxy potatoes

1 tsp salt

150 ml almond milk

1 pinch chilli flakes

¼ tsp garlic powder

1 tsp maple syrup

Juice of ½ lemon

200 ml vegetable stock

Salt and pepper

FOR THE ROASTED VEGETABLES

1 beetroot

1 golden beetroot

1 small parsnip

2 baby carrots

2 red onions

4 cloves garlic

1 tbsp olive oil

EXTRAS

2 tsp olive oil

METHOD

1 The previous day, put the almonds in a bowl, cover with plenty of cold water and soak overnight.

2 Preheat the oven to 180°C and line a baking tray with baking parchment.

3 Peel and quarter the potatoes. Boil the potatoes in a saucepan with sufficient water and then drain and leave to cool a little.

4 Trim and peel the beetroots, parsnip and carrots. Cut the beetroot into eighths and finely slice the parsnip. Peel and cut the onions into eighths. Peel the garlic. Place the vegetables on the tray, drizzle with the olive oil and roast in the hot oven (middle shelf) for 20–25 minutes.

5 Combine the cooked potatoes in a saucepan with the soaked almonds, almond milk, spices, lemon juice and vegetable stock, and bring to the boil. Then lower heat and blend to a creamy consistency with a hand-held blender. Before serving, bring the soup back to the boil and season with salt and pepper.

6 Divide the soup into two bowls, arrange the roasted vegetables on top and drizzle with a little olive oil.

 TIP

If you like a bit of heat, stir a pinch of chilli powder into the oil before you drizzle it over the vegetables.

30 MINUTES

20–25 MINUTES

FULL PROTEIN BOWL
WITH ROASTED AUBERGINE, SPINACH AND CHICKPEAS

INGREDIENTS

FOR THE VEGETABLES

1 aubergine – olive oil

¼ tsp ground turmeric

¼ tsp sweet paprika

1 pinch each of chilli powder
   and ground ginger

Salt

½ red onion

250 g baby spinach

1 tbsp maple syrup

Juice of ½ lemon

200 g cherry tomatoes

2 tbsp balsamic vinegar

FOR THE CHICKPEAS

1 tin chickpeas (about 240 g
   drained weight)

1 red onion

1 tbsp olive oil

¼ tsp ground coriander

¼ tsp garlic powder

Salt

EXTRAS

4 tbsp yoghurt dip
   (see page 22)

Garden cress

1 tbsp olive oil

METHOD

1 Preheat the oven to 180°C and line a baking tray with baking parchment.

2 Trim and wash the aubergine. Cut it in half lengthwise and score with a diamond pattern on the cut surface with a sharp knife. Make a marinade by mixing 1 tablespoon of olive oil with the turmeric, paprika, chilli, ginger and a pinch of salt. Brush the marinade over the cut surfaces of the aubergine and roast in the hot oven (middle shelf) for 30–40 minutes. In the meantime, drain the chickpeas from the tin, rinse and leave to drain. Peel and finely dice the onion. Put the chickpeas and onion into an ovenproof dish and mix them with the olive oil, spices and a pinch of salt. About 10 minutes before the aubergine finishes roasting, add the chickpeas to the tray and cook together.

3 Peel and finely dice the onion. Sort the spinach leaves, wash and shake dry. Heat a tablespoon of olive oil in a saucepan and sauté the onion with the maple syrup. Deglaze the pan with the lemon juice, reduce the heat to medium and add the spinach and 30 ml of water. Simmer for 4–5 minutes, stirring from time to time.

4 Wash and halve the cherry tomatoes. Heat a little olive oil in a frying pan, add the tomatoes and sauté for about 1 minute. Then deglaze the pan with the balsamic vinegar and 1 tablespoon of water, and simmer for 2–3 minutes. Season with salt.

5 Make the yoghurt dip as described on page 22. To serve, divide the vegetables and chickpeas into two shallow bowls. Top each bowl with 2 tablespoons of dip, sprinkle with a little garden cress and drizzle with olive oil.

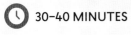 30–40 MINUTES

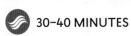 30–40 MINUTES

SQUASH RISOTTO BOWL
WITH FIGS AND WALNUTS

INGREDIENTS

250 g uchiki (red) kuri squash

4 tbsp olive oil

1 red onion

200 g risotto rice

475 ml white wine (or white balsamic vinegar)

2 tsp vegetable stock powder

2 tbsp yeast flakes

4 dried figs

40 g shelled walnuts

EXTRAS
1 fresh fig

Garden cress

METHOD

1 Preheat the oven to 180°C and line a baking tray with baking parchment.

2 Cut the squash in half, remove the seeds, dice the flesh and place in an ovenproof dish. Mix with 2 tablespoons of olive oil and roast in the hot oven (middle shelf) for 20–30 minutes.

3 In the meantime, peel and finely chop the onion. Put the risotto rice into a fine-mesh sieve and rinse under the tap until the water runs clear. Heat the remaining olive oil in a saucepan, add the onion and sauté for 2–3 minutes. Then add the rice and sauté until translucent. Deglaze the pan with the wine. After about 2 minutes, add 100 ml of water, the vegetable stock powder and yeast flakes. Simmer over a low heat, gradually adding about 350 ml more wine, until the risotto reaches the desired consistency.

4 In the meantime, cut the dried figs into small dice and coarsely chop the walnuts. Shortly before the risotto is finished cooking, mix in the figs, walnuts and squash cubes.

5 Wash and cut the figs into thin wedges. Divide the risotto into two bowls and garnish with the fresh fig wedges and a little garden cress before serving.

 30 MINUTES

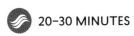 20–30 MINUTES

SQUASH BURGER BOWL

INGREDIENTS

FOR THE SQUASH BURGERS

50 g millet

Salt

250 g uchiki (red) kuri squash

Olive oil, for cooking

½ onion

1 clove garlic

1 tin haricot beans (about 240 g drained weight)

1 tsp maple syrup

Garden cress

Salt and pepper

FOR THE MUSTARD CREAM

150 g vegan yoghurt alternative (e.g. coconut), firm consistency

2 tbsp medium-strength mustard

1 tbsp maple syrup

Salt

EXTRAS

200 g lamb's lettuce

4 tbsp hummus (see page 20)

2 fresh figs

2 wholegrain bread rolls

METHOD

1 Preheat the oven to 180°C and line a baking tray with baking parchment. Put the millet into a fine-mesh sieve and rinse under the tap until the water runs clear. Then combine with about 250 ml of salted water in a saucepan and bring to the boil. Lower the heat and simmer for about 20 minutes, until all the liquid has been absorbed. Remove from the heat and keep warm.

2 Cut the squash in half, remove the seeds and cut the flesh into large chunks. Place the squash pieces on the tray, mix with 2 tablespoons of olive oil and roast in the hot oven (middle shelf) for 20–30 minutes. Then leave to cool a little. Cut a third of the squash into very thin strips and keep warm in the oven. Use a spoon to scoop the remainder of the flesh from the skin.

3 To make the mustard cream, mix all the ingredients together in a bowl and season with salt. Refrigerate to firm up the consistency of the cream.

4 Peel and finely chop the onion and garlic. Heat a little oil in a frying pan and sauté the onion and garlic until they turn translucent. Drain the beans from the tin, rinse and leave to drain. Then add them to the squash flesh and mash with a fork. Add the onion and garlic, millet, maple syrup and some of the cress, season with salt and pepper, and mix well. Shape the mixture into 2 large burgers to fit the size of the buns. Heat a little olive oil in a frying pan and fry the burgers on both sides for 2–3 minutes over medium heat, until golden brown.

5 Sort the lamb's lettuce, wash and shake dry. Make the hummus as described on page 20. Wash and slice the figs into thin strips. Cut the rolls in half across the middle and spread both halves with hummus. Put some lamb's lettuce on the bottom half and cover with the burgers. Spread a tablespoon of mustard cream over the top, garnish with figs and a couple of pumpkin strips, and cover with the lid. Divide the burgers together with the remaining lamb's lettuce and remaining pumpkin strips into two shallow bowls and drizzle with the remaining cream.

 55 MINUTES

 20-30 MINUTES

COLOURFUL ASIA BOWL
WITH PEANUT SAUCE

INGREDIENTS

1 courgette

2 carrots

1 yellow pepper

1 tsp coconut oil, for frying

120 g rice noodles

Salt

2 tbsp peanuts

FOR THE SAUCE

1 lime

1 clove garlic

1 small piece (about 1 cm) ginger

2 tbsp soy sauce

2 tsp peanut butter

1 tsp rice syrup

EXTRAS

2 tbsp roasted peanuts

½ lime

1 handful coriander

METHOD

1 To make the peanut sauce, squeeze the lime. Peel and very finely chop the garlic and ginger, and mix them with the remaining ingredients and a tablespoon of water to a creamy consistency.

2 Trim and wash the courgette. Trim and peel the carrots. Use a spiraliser to cut the courgette and carrots into noodle-like strips. Trim, wash and cut the pepper into thin strips.

3 Bring a sufficient amount of salted water to the boil in a saucepan. Steep the rice noodles for 4–5 minutes or cook them according to instructions on the packet, and then leave to drain. In a frying pan, heat the coconut oil and sauté the vegetables for 3–4 minutes over a medium heat.

4 Coarsely chop the peanuts and cut the lime into wedges. Wash the coriander, shake dry and pluck the leaves from the stems. Divide the rice noodles and vegetables into shallow bowls. Sprinkle everything with the peanuts and coriander leaves and serve with the lime wedges and peanut sauce.

 TIP

For people who are allergic to peanuts, they can be replaced in this dish with cashews and cashew butter for an equally delicious flavour.

CAULIFLOWER RICE BOWL
WITH CURRIED LENTILS

INGREDIENTS

FOR THE CAULIFLOWER RICE

500 g cauliflower

1 lemon

1 tsp coconut oil

½ tsp ground coriander

1 tsp maple syrup

Salt

FOR THE LENTILS

100 g red lentils

1 lime

½ onion

1 clove garlic

1 tsp coconut oil

½ tsp curry powder

½ tsp sweet paprika

¼ tsp ground coriander

1 pinch chilli flakes (optional)

Salt

1 tbsp maple syrup

1 tbsp almond butter

EXTRAS

1 carrot

1 handful coriander

2 tbsp flaked almonds

METHOD

1 Trim, wash and finely grate the cauliflower. Squeeze the lemon. Heat the coconut oil in a frying pan, then add the ground coriander, maple syrup and a pinch of salt, and toast for 1 minute. Deglaze the pan with the lemon juice and reduce the heat to medium heat. Add the grated cauliflower flakes and sauté for 15–20 minutes, stirring from time to time to keep from burning.

2 Put the lentils into a fine-mesh sieve and rinse under the tap until the water runs clear. Squeeze the lime. Peel and finely chop the onion and garlic. Heat the coconut oil in a saucepan, add the spices and a pinch of salt, and toast for about 1 minute, stirring constantly. Deglaze the pan with the lime juice and stir in the onion, garlic, maple syrup and almond butter, and briefly bring to the boil. Add the lentils and 250 ml of water, and bring back to the boil. Reduce the heat to medium and simmer for 10–12 minutes.

3 In the meantime, trim and peel the carrot. Use a spiraliser to cut it into thin ribbons. Wash the coriander, shake dry and pluck the leaves from the stems.

4 Divide the cauliflower rice into two shallow bowls. Top with the lentils and garnish with carrot ribbons, flaked almonds and fresh coriander.

30 MINUTES

DESSERT
BOWLS

FRUITY BERRY BOWL
WITH HAZELNUT BALLS

INGREDIENTS

FOR THE HAZELNUT BALLS

200 g pitted dates
  (e.g. Medjool)

100 g millet flakes

60 g hazelnuts

1 tbsp coconut oil

1–2 tbsp apple juice

4 tbsp hazelnut butter

Salt

EXTRAS

100 g redcurrants

100 g cherries

10 strawberries

60 g hazelnuts

METHOD

1   To make the hazelnut balls, combine all ingredients in a powerful blender and blend on low speed to form a sticky paste. If the paste becomes too dry, simply add another tablespoon of apple juice. Next, use wet hands to shape the paste into 18 balls of uniform size (with a diameter of about 2.5 cm).

2   Sort and wash the redcurrant clusters and carefully pat them dry. Then separate the berries. Remove the stems from the cherries and strawberries, then wash and cut them in half. Pit the cherries.

3   Arrange the fruits in two small bowls or one large one, and then place the hazelnut balls on top. Sprinkle with hazelnuts. This dish makes an excellent snack as well as a centrepiece dessert.

 TIP

You can sprinkle the dish with a tablespoon of baking cocoa for a chocolatey flavour. You can vary the fruits with the season and according to preference. For the ultimate chocolate sensation, the fruits can also be dipped in the cashew and chocolate spread (see recipe on page 23) – pure and sweet temptation!

30 MINUTES

BANANA DREAM BOWL
WITH CASHEW AND CHOCOLATE CREAM

INGREDIENTS

FOR THE BANANA BREAD
100 g ground almonds

100 g buckwheat flour

2 tsp Himalayan salt

4 small ripe bananas

100 ml almond milk

3 tbsp maple syrup

2 tbsp coconut oil

FOR THE CREAM
150 g cashew nuts

½ avocado

5 Medjool dates

3 tsp baking cocoa

125 ml almond milk

EXTRAS
30 x 11 cm loaf tin

30 g dark chocolate

METHOD

1 The previous day, put the cashews in a bowl, cover with plenty of cold water and soak overnight.

2 Preheat the oven to 180°C and line the loaf tin with baking parchment.

3 To make the banana bread, put all the dry ingredients into a bowl and add a pinch of salt. Peel 3 bananas, cut into large pieces and combine in a blender with the almond milk, maple syrup and coconut oil. Blend to a creamy consistency. Add the banana cream to the dry ingredients and mix with a hand mixer. Then pour the dough into the loaf tin. Halve the remaining banana lengthways and lay the halves cut side down on top of the batter. Bake in the hot oven (middle shelf) for 30–40 minutes, until golden brown.

4 In the meantime, make the cream. Drain the soaked cashews. Halve the avocado, remove the stone and scoop out the flesh. Pit the dates. Then combine all the ingredients in a blender and blend to a creamy consistency.

5 Coarsely chop the chocolate. Divide the cashew and chocolate cream into two small bowls. Cut the still warm banana bread into slices. Halve the slices and arrange them on top of the cream. Just before serving, dust with a tablespoon of chopped dark chocolate.

25 MINUTES

30–40 MINUTES

EASY COCONUT BOWL
WITH FRESH FIGS AND NUTS

INGREDIENTS

30 g shelled walnuts

1 fresh fig

300 g coconut yoghurt
alternative

3 tbsp maple syrup

2–4 mint leaves

METHOD

1   Coarsely chop the walnuts. Wash the fig, cut in half
lengthways and then into thin wedges.

2   Mix the coconut yoghurt alternative with 2 tablespoons of
water, then divide into two small bowls and garnish with
figs, walnuts, a little maple syrup and 1–2 mint leaves.

 TIP

Depending on the season, the figs can be replaced by other
fresh fruits, stewed fruits or compote. For example, a berry
compote or fresh peach wedges make a great summer dish,
while wintery apple wedges stewed with cinnamon are an ideal
way to round off Christmas dinner.

15 MINUTES

HOT AND COLD BOWL
WITH ESPRESSO PEARS AND WALNUT ICE CREAM

INGREDIENTS

2 pears

50 ml cold espresso coffee

Vegan walnut ice cream

METHOD

1 Wash and peel the pears. Put the cold espresso into a saucepan with 100 ml of water and the pears and bring to the boil, then reduce the heat to medium. Remove the pan from the heat after 5 minutes and leave the pears to steep for about 15 minutes, turning the pears occasionally.

2 Cool the steeped pears in the freezer for 5 minutes. Take the walnut ice cream out of the freezer and cut it into slices about 2 cm thick or use a scoop to make balls.

3 To serve, arrange an espresso pear and a slice or scoop of ice cream in each small bowl.

 TIP

If you don't like or can't have coffee, you can also use 2 cups of cold chai tea instead of espresso.

25 MINUTES

PLUM CAKE BOWL

INGREDIENTS

FOR THE PLUM CAKE

Coconut oil

8–10 plums

2 tsp ground cinnamon, plus a little more for finishing

1 tsp ground fennel

½ tsp ground star anise

¼ tsp ground cloves

Sea salt and pepper

280 g wholemeal spelt flour

2½ tsp baking powder

150 ml maple syrup

200 ml almond milk

FOR THE CREAM

200 g vegan yoghurt alternative (e.g. coconut, almond, soya)

3 tbsp maple syrup

1 tsp lemon juice

METHOD

1 Preheat the oven to 180°C and grease one large or six small ovenproof dishes with coconut oil.

2 Wash, halve and de-stone the plums. Cut them into thin wedges. Cover the bottom of the large or small dishes with about two-thirds of the plum wedges.

3 Combine the spices with a pinch each of sea salt and pepper in a small bowl and mix with the flour and baking powder.

4 Heat 3 tablespoons of coconut oil in a frying pan over low heat. Stir in the maple syrup and almond milk, warm briefly and then mix with dry ingredients to a smooth batter. Pour the batter over the plums, top with the remaining plum wedges and bake in the hot oven (middle shelf) for 35–40 minutes, until golden brown.

5 In the meanwhile, mix the yoghurt alternative with the maple syrup and lemon juice to a smooth and creamy consistency.

6 Take the cake or cakes out of the oven and leave to cool for about 15 minutes. Top each cake or individual portion with a tablespoon of cream and a pinch of cinnamon before serving.

 20 MINUTES

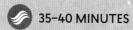 35–40 MINUTES

VERY BERRY CRUMBLE BOWL

INGREDIENTS

FOR THE CRUMBLE

2 apples

1 lemon

2 tbsp maple syrup

750 g frozen mixed berries

100 g millet flakes

60 g puffed amaranth

40 g cornmeal

2 tbsp maple syrup

2 tbsp coconut oil, plus a
little more for greasing

FOR THE CREAM

200 g vegan yoghurt
alternative (e.g. coconut,
almond, soy)

¼ tsp Bourbon vanilla powder

2 tbsp maple syrup

METHOD

1 Preheat the oven to 160 °C and grease four small or two
large ovenproof dishes with coconut oil.

2 Wash, halve and core the apples. Cut them into small
bite-sized chunks. Squeeze the lemon and mix the juice
with the maple syrup.

3 Mix the frozen berries with the apple pieces in the
prepared dishes and mix well with the syrup and juice
mixture.

4 Mix the millet flakes, puffed amaranth and cornmeal in a
bowl, then add the maple syrup and coconut oil and rub
in well to form crumbs. Spread the crumble evenly over
the fruit in the dishes and bake in the hot oven (middle
shelf) for 30–40 minutes, until golden brown.

5 In the meantime, make the cream by mixing the yoghurt
alternative with the vanilla and maple syrup.

6 Take the crumble out of the oven and leave to cool a little.
Serve while still warm, with each dish topped with a
tablespoon of cream.

 TIP

This fruity bowl also makes a wonderfully warming breakfast on
cold days.

15 MINUTES

30-40 MINUTES

MOUNTAIN LODGE BOWL
WITH TORN BUCKWHEAT PANCAKES

INGREDIENTS

FOR THE PANCAKES

1 banana

1 tsp chia seeds

200 ml almond milk

3 tbsp maple syrup

40 g buckwheat flour

70 g spelt flour

½ tsp baking powder

½ tsp ground cinnamon

Salt

1 tsp coconut oil, for cooking

EXTRAS

½ lemon

1 large apple

2 tbsp flaked almonds

1 tbsp maple syrup

Ground cinnamon

150 g apple purée

METHOD

1 Peel and mash the banana in a bowl with a fork. Add the chia seeds, almond milk and maple syrup and incorporate. In a second bowl, mix the flours with the baking powder and a pinch each of cinnamon and salt. Then fold the dry ingredients into the banana mixture to make a thick batter.

2 Heat the coconut oil in a frying pan and pour in the batter. Reduce the heat to low and cook the pancake for 5–6 minutes. Then turn it over and cook for 4–5 more minutes, until golden brown.

3 In the meantime, squeeze the lemon. Wash the apple, quarter, core and cut into small dice. In a small saucepan, combine the diced apple, lemon juice, flaked almonds, maple syrup, a pinch of cinnamon and 2 tablespoons of water, and cook over a medium heat for 4–5 minutes, stirring constantly. Add a little more water if necessary.

4 Season the apple purée with a pinch of cinnamon. Use two forks to tear the pancake into small pieces and divide them into two shallow bowls. Pour the warm apple and almond mixture over the top. Add a dollop of apple purée to each bowl or serve separately in a small bowl.

 TIP

You can also use mango pulp instead of the apple purée and replace the cinnamon with a tablespoon of coconut flakes.

30 MINUTES

INDEX

ACKNOWLEDGEMENTS

Today, when I think back on all my culinary journeys through the foods of different countries, restaurants and market explorations that inspired me to write this book, I can't help but smile from ear to ear. I would like to thank my friend Manuel, who has always guided me with his fine palate. Thanks also go to my friend Stefanie, who showed me the diversity of the vegan diet several years ago. Thank you. Heartfelt thanks also go to my editor Diana and the publishers EMF-Verlag, who made this project possible, as well as Bernadette, who took care of the wonderful design of this book. Thank you to all the amazing people who put heart and soul into making this book possible and to Grub Street for the English edition.

ABOUT THE AUTHOR

Jessica Lerchenmüller loves to travel and explore the cuisines of foreign countries for the readers of her culinary blog (www.vollmundig.org). She invites you to try her modern and inspirational recipes. Fresh, healthy ingredients and amazing spices are an important part of the nutritional philosophy behind them. This native of the Austria's Vorarlberg region is passionate about cooking for her friends and inspiring them with her simple but creative style in the kitchen. Her camera, notebook and pencil are constant companions.

This English language edition published in 2022 by

Grub Street
4 Rainham Close
London
SW11 6SS

Email: food@grubstreet.co.uk
Twitter: @grub_street
Facebook: Grub Street Publishing
Web: www.grubstreet.co.uk

Copyright this English language edition © Grub Street 2022
First published in German as Buddha Bowls Vegan
This translation published by arrangement with Silke Bruenink
Agency, Munich, Germany
© 2021 Edition Michael Fischer GmbH
Cover design and layout: Bernadett Linseisen
Layout: Lara Nelles and Carolin Mayer
Photos: Jessica Lerchenmüller, Dornbirn; except pages 10–25
Nadja Buchczik, Bielefeld

A CIP record for this title is available from the British Library

ISBN 978-1-911667-33-9

The statements and advice published in the book have been
carefully prepared and checked by the author and the publisher.
However, no guarantee can be given for their success, nor can
the author or the publisher and their representatives be held
liable for personal injury, property damage or financial loss.

All rights reserved. No part of this book may be reproduced
or transmitted in any form or by any means, electronic or
mechanical, including photocopying, recording or any
information storage and retrieval system, without permission
in writing from the publisher.

Printed and bound by Print Best, Estonia